A Guide to Curriculum Planning in Reading

Doris M. Cook
Supervisor,
Reading Education (retired)

Wisconsin Department of Public Instruction
Madison, Wisconsin

This publication is available from:

Publication Sales
Wisconsin Department of Public Instruction
P.O. Box 7841
Madison, WI 53707-7841
(800) 243-8782

Bulletin No. 6305

© 1986 Wisconsin Department of Public Instruction

Approved for reprint 1993, 1995.

ISBN 1-57337-014-2

Printed on
Recycled Paper

Contents of the Guide

7 Organizing for Instruction

8 Selecting Instructional Materials

9 Evaluating the Reading Curriculum

10 Contributors to an Effective Reading Program

11 Appendixes

A Guide to Curriculum Planning in Reading is part of the Department of Public Instruction's ongoing efforts to provide assistance and support to local school districts in the development of comprehensive K-12 reading programs.

Reading is defined as a dynamic interactive process involving the reader in constructing meaning. The definition is illustrated in the Wisconsin Model for Reading Comprehension found in section 2 and is the basis for this guide.

It is clear from the work of the National Commission on Reading that efforts can be made to improve the effectiveness of reading instruction. According to the Commission's report, *Becoming a Nation of Readers,* "The knowledge is now available to make worthwhile improvements in reading throughout the United States. If the practices seen in the classrooms of the best teachers in the best schools could be introduced everywhere the improvements in reading would be dramatic."

It is certainly our hope that this guide can be a valuable resoource and reference and contribute substantially to our becoming a state and nation of readers.

John T. Benson
State Superintendent

A Guide to Curriculum Planning in Reading would not have been possible without the efforts of many individuals.

The Reading Task Force members gave freely of their time and expertise in drafting the guide. Their employing agencies were generous in granting them time to work on the publication. Task Force members are

Marleen Anklam
K-5 Language Arts Coordinator and Teacher
Edgerton Community Elementary School
Edgerton School District

Judith Casey
Administrator
Stone Bank School District

Lowell Gillette
Reading Specialist and Projects
  Coordinator
Cooperative Educational Service Agency #11

Jane Greenewald
Reading Education Professor
University of Wisconsin-LaCrosse

Mary Jett-Simpson
Reading Education Professor
Department of Curriculum and Instruction
University of Wisconsin-Milwaukee

Frances Kimmey (retired)
Reading Specialist and Curriculum
  Consultant
Department of Public Instruction

Pat Norman
Assistant Principal and Reading
  Specialist
New Richmond School District

Robert Pavlik
Director of Reading-Learning Programs
Chair of Reading-Language Arts
  Department
Cardinal Stritch College, Milwaukee

Doug Vance
Reading Specialist
LaFollette High School
Madison Metropolitan School District

Charles Wedig
Elementary Principal
Deerfield Community School District

Special appreciation is extended to other educators and classroom teachers who provided valuable contributions and constructive criticism as the guide was being developed. They include Doug Buehl, Madison East High School; Velma Dauer, Edgerton Public Schools; Jean Frost, Muskego-Norway Schools; Dale Johnson, Boston University; Martha Kinney, University of Wisconsin-Superior; Nancy Kirchberg, Columbus Public Schools; Marjorie Lipson, University of Vermont; Nikki Mason, Columbus Public Schools; Joy Monahan, Orange County Schools, Orlando, Florida; Wayne Otto, University of Wisconsin-Madison; Joe Papenfus, Racine Public Schools; Walter Prentice, University of Wisconsin-Superior; Nancy Runkle, Waukesha Public Schools; Carol Santa, Kalispel, Montana; Mary Lou Sharpee, Columbus Public Schools; Richard Sorensen, DPI; and Martin Rayala, DPI.

A special thanks to members of the Department of Public Instruction who offered suggestions as the guide was being developed: Russ Allen, Elaine Anderson, Ben Brewer, Eunice Bethke, Frank Evans, Ellen Last, Betty VanderSchaaf, and Norm Webb. Finally, gratitude is extended to Pat Arnold, Amy French, Connie Haas, Neldine Nichols, Mary Parks, Telise Johnsen, Vickie Rettenmund, Jane Lepeska, Jill Howman, and Patty Venner for their help in the preparation of the guide.

Doris M. Cook
Supervisor, Reading Education

Overview 1

Introduction to the Guide

Good curriculum documents are the foundation for successful curriculum implementation. They are not an end in themselves, but are the means to an end.

A Guide to Curriculum Planning in Reading is addressed to groups and individuals who are responsible for planning and providing effective reading instruction in elementary and secondary schools. The guide presents an instructional framework for reading education to assist local district reading committees in curriculum development or revision. It can also be used as a resource for staff development programs and as a reference for teachers in lesson planning.

The purposes of the guide are
● to establish a definition of reading comprehension as an interactive process;
● to facilitate effective and creative decision making by teachers for
  – integrating reading and writing across the curriculum;
  – developing readers who can independently apply appropriate strategies to a variety of texts and tasks for constructing meaning;
  – developing mature readers who will choose reading as an independent activity during and beyond their school years.

Reading Comprehension as Focus. The last few years have brought significant changes in understanding reading comprehension. Reading is now regarded as an active search for meaning rather than as a mechanical translation of the written code. The guide describes an appropriate curriculum for developing the interactive nature of comprehension and provides guidance for implementing a K-12 reading curriculum which emphasizes comprehension.

Integrating Reading with the Language Arts. The integration of reading with the language arts, especially writing, is stressed. Section 4 provides a K-12 scope and sequence, and section 7 offers an organizational plan for integrating reading and the language arts in the elementary grades and provides suggested activities for incorporating writing across the curriculum in all content areas. Additionally, help can be gotten from *A Guide to Curriculum Planning in the Language Arts.*

Developing Strategic Readers. The goal of developing strategic behavior, that which enables students to independently apply various techniques in reading, is emphasized throughout the guide. An instructional framework and model lessons for developing strategic readers are found in section 3.

Secondary Reading. The development of independent, skillful readers is a never-ending process. This notion offers a challenge to secondary teachers who may have assumed that their students have acquired all the necessary skills for reading and learning new content. This guide, with its emphasis on *reader, text,* and *context,* implies that continuing reading instruction needs to occur in all subject areas throughout high school. All sections address secondary reading.

Reading for Enjoyment. Reports of the National Assessment of Educational Progress (1982 and 1985) indicate that most students do not enjoy reading or choose it for gaining personal information. Section 4 outlines a scope and sequence for teachers to use to model affective reading behaviors and to provide opportunities for students to choose reading at all stages and in all subject areas.

Teachers as Decision Makers. Finally, the guide presents a challenge to teachers to create a new classroom environment. It presents a blend of current research in reading and teacher effectiveness and provides specific suggestions to aid teachers to assume an increasingly active, positive role by
● spending more classroom time teaching students how to comprehend;
● encouraging students to activate their existing knowledge as an aid to comprehension;
● providing guided practice and appropriate reading materials for developing independence in the use of strategies;
● teaching students to use the organizing features of text as an aid to comprehension;
● modeling and encouraging students to monitor their own comprehension;
● modeling the enjoyment of reading and providing time for self-selected reading;
● using writing as an informal learning tool during and after reading.

While some of the ideas and concepts in this guide are already part of reading instruction in many classrooms, other concepts are new and will require local educators to study this guide and current research before they attempt to incorporate them into their program. The task force hopes that as districts implement the ideas contained in the guide, teachers and students will enjoy reading and writing more and will value reading and writing as essential tools for improving literacy.

The annotated bibliography, Appendix N, includes the references used to develop this guide. Users of the guide should find the bibliography helpful in assessing their current programs.

Curriculum Development Process in Reading

A Guide to Curriculum Planning in Reading is designed to assist local school district staff who share responsibility for the development and updating of a comprehensive K–12 reading curriculum. Most districts are in some phase of refining reading curriculum each year whether pilot testing, evaluating new textbooks and supplementary materials, implementing new ideas, or rewriting current reading program guides. An exemplary reading curriculum is an ongoing documentation of possibilities for change. It outlines the overall K-12 program yet allows for additions and innovations that will keep a reading program current. This insight is important because, as the result of research which has been conducted over the past ten years, the development and act of reading comprehension are being substantially reconceptualized.

The general steps of the process for all curriculum development are outlined in detail in a companion to this document, *A Guide to Curriculum Planning*, while this guide addresses the specific concerns for developing a K-12 reading curriculum. Particular attention is given to functions of reading specialists.

At the heart of the current emphasis on educational excellence is a new priority on curriculum development.

Committee Organization

The reading curriculum development process begins with the selection of a committee. Successful curriculum development depends upon the involvement and support of K-12 classroom teachers, reading specialists, school administrators, parents, and students. In most districts, the superintendent appoints a coordinator, usually the school district's reading specialist, who can organize the committee, act as liaison between administrators and the committee, and provide leadership for the entire process.

Curriculum Development Steps

A first step for the reading committee is to review *A Guide to Curriculum Planning in Reading* and the related research, considering the implications for the district. The following questions will be helpful for the committee to discuss as it examines the issues which are explored in the guide and the research.

• What does recent research say about the teaching and learning of reading?

• How should comprehension as an interactive process be taught?

• What are the characteristics of a strategic reader?

• What is the teacher's role in developing strategic readers?

• What attitudes and values should students acquire to become life-long readers?

• What kinds of staff development are needed to help teachers assume the role of active decision makers?

• What opportunities, materials, and resources are essential for providing a wide variety of reading experiences?

• What evaluative procedures can be used to measure a reading curriculum in terms of students' present and future needs?

After reviewing the guide and the research, the reading specialist and the committee must then develop a plan and timeline for completing the following tasks.

- Examine existing program
- Review present comprehension competencies of students
- Identify goals of reading curriculum
- Select objectives for accomplishing goals
- Choose materials to implement goals and objectives
- Pilot test changes in proposed curriculum
- Write new curriculum
- Present new curriculum to district staff and board of education
- Plan appropriate staff development activities

Philosophy—Goals—Competencies

After the committee has reviewed the research, it needs to formulate a philosophy and set broad program goals. Statements of philosophy and goals give direction to those responsible for planning, implementing, and evaluating the district curriculum. Both philosophy and goals should reflect and be consistent with the overall philosophy and goals of the school district.

A statement of philosophy clarifies the direction for the reading curriculum development effort. It justifies the inclusion of K-12 reading instruction in the curriculum, ties reading to educational performance, and delineates the expectations for student accomplishment.

The reading curriculum committee can draw on many sources to adapt a philosophy statement to guide its work in curriculum development. The Basic Considerations (table 1) developed by the task force served as the philosophy statement for the development of *A Curriculum Planning in Reading*. Local districts may wish to adapt this to fit local needs or to use as a starting point for developing their own philosophy.

Goal statements are derived from the philosophy and reflect the ultimate outcomes of instruction. These statements encourage the use of broad-gauged measures for assessing the reading curriculum, serve as an impetus for constant program improvement, and give direction for further curriculum development. The goals are also helpful in communicating to parents and the community.

Once a philosophy has been written and broad goals established, specific outcomes for students need to be stated. These outcomes may be stated as competencies which are expected as a result of the curriculum and instruction. School districts often view these competencies as a yardstick for measuring the success of the total reading program.

... educational objectives that reflect the interaction of reader, text and process rather than definitions of discrete units that can be directly translated into observable behaviors. –NAEP, 1985

An Effective Reading Program:
Basic Considerations

READING is comprehension. Reading comprehension is a dynamic interactive process of constructing meaning by combining the reader's existing knowledge with the text information within the context of the reading situation. The key elements are reader, text, *and* context.

The major goal of an effective reading program is the development of strategic readers who are knowledgeable about the reading act and who
- construct meaning from print
- apply strategies to learn from text
- develop an interest in reading as a life-long enjoyment

Strategic Readers
- analyze reading task
- establish reading purpose
- plan appropriate strategies

- monitor understanding while reading
- regulate by making appropriate corrections
- reflect upon task at completion

Reading is a developmental process where students progress at their own rate.

Effective reading instruction is student centered. It
- teaches students what they need to know, not what they already know
- builds upon background knowledge

Teachers are professional decision makers who decide how and what to teach. They
- plan lessons using a variety of materials
- model appropriate reading behaviors by
  - demonstrating effective strategies
  - reading aloud to students
  - encouraging students to interact
- organize flexible groups for varied instructional purposes

An effective reading program is more than a basal. It
- includes a variety of materials
  - narrative
  - expository
- encourages self selection

Reading instruction encompasses the entire curriculum across all content areas. It
- requires both general and specific reading objectives
  - learning to read text (process)
  - gaining specific information (content)
- integrates language arts instruction with content
  - reading, writing, and discussing
  - clarifying and organizing thinking

An effective lesson includes pre-reading, reading, and post-reading activities. Teachers
- determine reading situation
- identify what students know
- identify what students need to learn
- model teaching
- demonstrate guided practice
- provide appropriate independent activities
- translate application to familiar and new reading situations

Comprehension is the main event of reading instruction. Teachers
- utilize background knowledge
- develop thinking and reasoning skills
- emphasize strategic behavior

The goal of teaching word analysis is meaning. Teachers
- base teaching of skills on assessed needs
- teach skills in context
- provide practice leading to automaticity

Effective instruction moves the student from dependence to independence. Mature readers learn to
- set purposes for reading
- adapt rate to purpose
- organize the reading task
- expand vocabulary
- monitor comprehension
- reflect on reading
- apply effective strategies to all reading situations

Reading is the best practice for learning to read. Teachers
- provide opportunity to automatize skills
- require time for silent reading
- encourage reading for varying purposes
- assure students the opportunity to interact with others
- motivate further reading

The development of positive attitudes toward reading will result in students who can and do read.

Staff development is an essential component of a reading program. Reading specialists
- keep teachers abreast of new research;
- demonstrate application of research findings;
- establish a viable rationale for textbook selection;
- plan continuous staff development.

An example of how competencies are derived from program goals follows. The competencies reflect the goals and curriculum described in this guide. Local curriculum committees may use these competency statements as a guide for determining their own.

Goals

Effective reading instruction develops strategic readers who are knowledgeable about the reading act and who can
- construct meaning from print;
- apply strategies to learn from text;
- develop an interest in reading as a life-long enjoyment.

Competencies

- Students will demonstrate knowledge about reading.
  - Know that background and skills influence comprehension
  - Know how different types of text and text features aid comprehension
  - Know the demands of various reading tasks
  - Know that comprehension requires an interaction among reader, text, and task

- Students can construct meaning from print.
  - Comprehend various types of print material
  - Comprehend materials read for a specific purpose

- Students can apply strategies to learn from text.
  - Select strategies appropriate for given text, task, and purpose
  - Use appropriate strategies under varying situations (text, task, purpose) to learn from text

- Students develop an interest in reading as a means of life-long enjoyment.
  - Demonstrate a positive attitude toward reading and toward self as a reader
  - Choose to read both at home and in school
  - Read a variety of materials for different purposes

Understanding Reading Comprehension as an Interactive Process

2

Wisconsin Model for Reading Comprehension

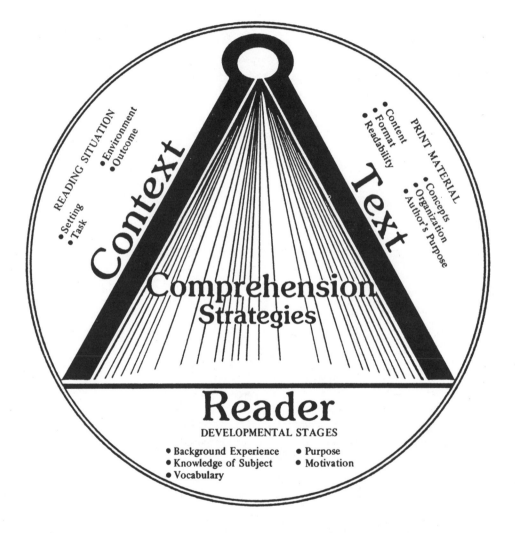

Recent research on the reading process has increased our understanding of how people derive meaning when reading. This research has led to the construction of an interactive model for reading comprehension involving the *reader*, the *text*, and the *context* (see figure 1). The triadic model represents the theoretical basis for this curriculum guide and serves as the organizing principle in each section. It helps to confirm that reading is a dynamic interactive process and that reading comprehension is holistic and includes more than a set of isolated skills.

Reading comprehension is determined by the following.
- What the *reader* brings to the act of reading comprehension
- Ways the printed *text* has been written and organized by the author
- The learning *context* that defines the task and purpose of the reader and the reading environment
- *Strategies* the reader consciously applies to achieve comprehension

Reading is accomplished through interactive rather than sequential processes.
–Rumelhart (1977)

The research on reading during the past decade has focused on *how* comprehension takes place and *what* students comprehend (Anderson, Osborne and Tierney, 1984; Pearson, 1984). This view represents a process approach rather than the acquisition of a set of skills (Duffy, Roehler, and Mason, 1984). Understanding reading as a process has many practical implications for instruction. Where traditionally the emphasis has been on a series of discrete skills, the new view focuses on the inter-related, ongoing activity of the learning itself. How reading comprehension is achieved becomes just as important as what is read or when it is assigned. The various traditional skills involved in reading are perceived as a means to an end—the ability of a reader to comprehend—rather than as goals in themselves.

Reading comprehension involves an *active communication* between the writer and reader within meaningful contexts. It is presumed that an author has an audience, a message, and a purpose in mind. These components may shift within a single book or article. Readers need to recognize the author's intent as well as the meaning. By integrating material received from the text with what they already know, readers create new concepts in their minds. The comprehension process is thus active and dynamic, with readers making inferences, accommodating new understanding to previous learning, and adjusting reading rate and strategies to varying requirements of the text, the reading context, and the purpose for reading (Langer and Smith-Burke, 1982).

Reader

The Wisconsin Model illustrated in figure 1 highlights the importance of the reader. Readers approach a given reading task having varying experiences and knowledge about the text, the topic, sense of purpose, and levels of motivation (Anderson, Osborne, Tierney, 1984). Comprehension involves connecting text material with facts, concepts, and beliefs already held by the reader and ordering the information into categories variously termed frames, scripts, or schema (Anderson and Pearson, 1984).

These categories or schema refer to the specific experiences, beliefs, and information that one brings to a given reading task. For example, a student knowing something about hot rods or computers is likely to read in those areas with greater comprehension than those without such knowledge. Less obvious is that a student with acquired information concerning, say, the geography of Latin America is likely to be more motivated and achieve greater comprehension from a story set in Bolivia.

The reader's purpose will vary with both the material and the task at hand, and will determine the strategies to be utilized. The student who needs only to fill in a worksheet will read differently from one having chosen a book for personal information and entertainment. If the assigned task is to receive the author's general idea, skimming may suffice. A more complete understanding would require careful scrutiny of the text. If the material is to be remembered in detail, underlining or note taking may be considered necessary. The strategic reader has the ability to apply appropriate strategies for each reading situation.

Text

Text is any print material that contains meaning. It commonly includes basal readers, subject area textbooks, fiction and nonfiction trade books and paperbacks, and articles from newspapers and magazines. There are, of course, other forms of printed matter, which teachers may wish to use, including personal correspondence and messages on television, signs, and bulletin boards. Texts differ widely in content, structure, style, and the writer's intent, which may be to inform, persuade, or entertain, or some combination of the three.

Whatever the text, it needs to be organized and written in a manner designed to communicate ideas and information, and to provide the basis for a collaboration between the writer and reader. If not, the text will be incomprehensible to even a capable reader.

Student readers are confronted with materials that may vary a great deal in level of difficulty. In the past, readability formulas have been used to determine the difficulty of a given text (Klare, 1984). Recent research indicates that readability scores are misleading since the formulas are almost always based on the limited criteria of word length and sentence length. This research has led to updated criteria for selecting appropriate reading material which emphasizes text style and coherence.

Instructional reading material that is well organized, coherent, and appropriate for its intended audience is called *considerate text* (Anderson and Armbruster, 1984). By definition, such material is designed to help the student learn the ideas and information contained in the writing. The text is clearly and reasonably arranged and includes introductions and summaries, effective headings, and helpful study guides such as diagrams, definitions, and questions. The writing style is clear, logical, and consistent. The text reflects an awareness of the knowledge base of students for whom it is designed, providing adequate explanations whenever new material is presented. Meyer (1981) has shown that stories that follow traditional story structure are easier for young readers to understand and remember than others with a similar vocabulary level but an unorganized structure. Children's understanding of story structure can aid comprehension (Stein and Glenn, 1979; Whaley, 1981). By learning how texts are organized, students can begin to adjust their strategies and effectively monitor their own comprehension (Meyer and Rice, 1984).

Context

Reading comprehension is not only dependent on the characteristics of the reader and the text but also on the context, or reading environment. A student is likely to read differently in a busy classroom than in a quiet place at home. The context for reading also includes the reader's purpose, the task, the expectations of the teacher, and the perceived result or use of reading. In addition, the makeup of the reading group, the classroom atmosphere, and the interactions with the teacher are important in setting the context for reading (Duffy, Roehler, Mason, 1984).

The task or reading assignment includes the choice of material, the amount of preteaching of vocabulary and concepts, the clarity of objectives, and the knowledge of purpose. Students' comprehension will vary greatly according to their understanding of the task and their purposes for reading. For example, if they know they will be tested, students will employ different strategies than if they are expected to discuss the issue. The entire learning situation, including peer attitudes and capabilities, affects the reading achievement of students.

The students' home environments can be crucial to developing reading comprehension. If their homes contain books and other reading materials as well as adults who read, students are more likely to value reading and choose it as an activity. However, parents who are not readers but value and encourage that activity can help provide the necessary motivation to their children.

Strategies

There has been a conceptual shift in the way many researchers and teachers think about reading which gives students a much more active role in the learning and reading comprehension process. This shift is reflected in changes from packaged reading programs to experiences with books and from concentration on isolated skills to practical reading and writing activities.
–Reading Report Card NAEP (1985)

Readers can improve their comprehension by employing effective strategies. Strategic reading involves analyzing the reading task, establishing a purpose for reading, and then selecting and using strategies for accomplishing the purpose (Paris, Lipson, Wixson, 1983). Strategies are self-directed plans for comprehending print material and require that the reader be knowledgeable about reading as a thinking activity as well as having control over the actual reading behavior. For example, a reader might skim, scan, or preview the headings to get a feel for the text. During the actual reading, readers might take notes, underline, or use a mapping technique to help remember the information. The important point is that the reader is aware of the purpose for reading and how employing various strategies will achieve that purpose.

Students need to know how to monitor their degree of comprehension. If the reading material is difficult, students should recognize when they don't understand and know how to use corrective strategies such as rereading to correct the problem. When the reading is completed, students need to know how to reflect on what they have read.

In summary, strategic reading behavior includes the ability to

- analyze the reading task;
- establish a purpose;
- plan appropriate strategies;
- monitor understanding while reading;
- regulate by making appropriate corrections;
- reflect upon task at completion.

Developing Strategic Readers

3

Introduction

The model for comprehension (figure 1) highlights the importance of readers and what they bring to the reading situation.

Reading development is a process of growth and change. The process varies among individuals due to physical growth, outside interests, attitudes toward reading and learning, and previous experiences. The nature of the process alters as readers mature. Changes occur in what individuals can do, and these changes help determine what they are expected to do. The ability and motivation to become an independent, self-directed reader occur in stages over a long period of time.

Stages describe the progress in reading from the very early emerging stage to the most advanced levels. The idea of stages of reading growth is not new. Both Gates (1925) and Gray (1939) wrote that reading instruction should be planned with stages in mind so that appropriate experiences could be provided at each developmental stage. Chall (1983) confirmed a developmental process that serves as the format for the developmental stages of reading described in this guide.

An important value of stage development theory is the emphasis on broad characteristics of readers and the related qualitative changes that occur. Since reading development is a process continuing all through life, the reading skills are never fully mastered but are refined as a reader progresses through the stages. The reading curriculum should be spiral in nature, providing continuing opportunities for each reader to progress by reading and comprehending increasingly complex materials. An understanding of stage development theory gives teachers a perspective as to how their instruction fits into a larger pattern of growth. School districts that use stages to organize their reading curriculum will want to provide each classroom teacher with a copy of the entire description of stages to help them develop a fuller understanding of where readers are, where they have been, and what instruction will move them forward.

Developmental Stages of Reading

The stages portrayed in figure 2 and explained below suggest characteristics of a reader at various stages. Background knowledge and vocabulary are essential at all stages and are continuously developed and refined through a variety of experiences and wide reading. The stage descriptors and characteristics need to be thought of as general guidelines. The stages cannot be accurately defined by grade level since students in a single class could be at varying stages, depending upon the task, the text, and the students' experiences. The ultimate goal of creating independent readers should be kept in mind at all stages for all teaching activities. During early stages students are more dependent upon their teachers or parents. With proper guidance and instruction, students move from dependence to independence (Vygotsky, 1978). Teachers at every level should encourage and expect independence in tasks appropriate for that stage of development.

Emergent Reading. The Emergent Reading stage is characterized by natural, unstructured learning. The emergent readers engage in a variety of language tasks determined to a great extent by their immediate environment (context). The relationship between children and their environments is emulative rather than instructional. Modeling and reinforcement shape much of young children's learning in language as well as in other behavior. An initial exploration of print through imitative writing, drawing, and questioning occurs at this stage.

The analysis of the individual differences is at the heart of the educational process.
—J. Orasanu (1985)

Beginning Reading. The Beginning Reading stage is characterized by the young reader tackling the written language system. The environment which remains important is likely to include an instructor and text, although the former may be a parent and the latter a storybook. As youngsters are thoughtfully introduced to functional written language and as they are encouraged to use their previously developed language learning strategies, they begin to learn the formal spelling patterns. This stage is characterized by gaining decoding skills for determining the meaning of unfamiliar words. As beginning readers generalize these rules, they also monitor their decoding by checking to see if what they read makes sense.

Reading for Consolidation. The Reading for Consolidation stage is characterized by the fluency readers now have in identifying unfamiliar words and predicting their meaning. Both of these skills should be done automatically at this stage. Also readers are learning to recognize the various text structures including the characteristics of stories and the organization of informational books. These readers enjoy reading in a variety of settings, and they use their prior knowledge and experiences to pursue individual interests in reading.

Reading to Learn the New. Reading to Learn the New is characterized by readers adapting to changes in the kinds of text read and the purposes for reading. Prior to this stage, familiar topics were used in the instructional materials to aid comprehension. As unfamiliar subjects and different kinds of texts make different demands on them, readers at this stage are able to tackle a range of reading materials for different purposes, use background knowledge to aid in comprehension, and apply some general strategies for remembering information.

Reading for Independence. Reading for Independence is the stage in which readers refine their abilities to work with subject matter. Readers are now more aware of text style and organization and can use text features as an aid in comprehension or remembering. They can analyze the task and determine appropriate strategies. Readers at this stage can be expected to evaluate more than one viewpoint, consider opposing evidence, and integrate a variety of research material.

Mature Reading. Mature readers can reconstruct meanings or shape ideas for their own uses. Readers at this stage are capable of dealing with a high level of abstraction. Reading strategies are independently applied to difficult and complex texts to meet the demands of their personal and career situations. They read in order to gain new information or insights from others and create new viewpoints and generalizations.

Strategic Reading Behavior

Research during the past decade has expanded on what it means to be a skilled reader. It has become increasingly clear that reading is a complex cognitive activity that is dynamic and constructive in nature. The recognition that skilled reading requires active engagement on the part of the reader has led researchers and educators to reconsider the characteristics of effective reading behavior. The understanding of reading as an interactive process means that the focus should no longer be upon the text as a static entity to be learned nor upon certain specific skills being acquired in an exact order according to a specific timetable. Since the process is variable, the reader must be prepared to employ a repertoire of skills flexibly to meet the situation. When such a model of reading is adopted, the act becomes quite similar to other human activities like thinking and problem solving. Indeed, many of today's reading professionals have adopted information processing models because they imply that the goal of reading is to to accommodate and assimilate the textual information into existing knowledge structures.

As researchers have tried to learn more about the reading process, they have attempted to characterize expert behavior. What do expert readers do when they encounter print? Accounts of expert-novice differences in a wide variety of situations (including memory tasks, problem-solving tasks, and listening-reading tasks) suggest that one of the things that differentiates experts from novices is the level of metacognition (Brown, 1978; Flavell, 1978). These authors note that experts are more aware of the *person, task,* and *strategy* dimensions that may affect performance. Others have called these metacognitive behaviors *planning, evaluation, monitoring,* and *regulation* (Paris & Lindauer, 1982). Although the terminology may vary, most authors agree that meta-cognition includes two critical dimensions: knowledge about cognition and control over cognition. Expert readers know more about what is required to read effectively, and they are better able to control their reading-related behaviors (August, Flavell and Clift, 1984; Armbruster, Echols, and Brown, 1983; Baker and Brown, 1984).

The broad goal of reading, of course, is to achieve understanding of the text, yet the level of understanding depends upon the reader's purpose. Since reading purposes vary, the criteria used to measure understanding or comprehension must vary as well. The context within which the reading act occurs is a part of that act. In some situations, for example, the reader may need to comprehend material in close detail for the purpose of passing an examination. In others the same reader may need only to comprehend the gist of a passage and so will skim it rather than deliberately read it. In self-monitoring, strategic readers will be referring constantly back to their original purposes.

Not surprisingly, poor readers appear less strategic than good readers (Forrest and Waller, 1979; Paris and Myers, 1981; Ryan, 1981). While strategic behavior is clearly developmental (older children are better than younger children and adults are better than both), it is equally clear that less able readers do not acquire the knowledge and control necessary to improve their performance. There are many reasons that younger and less able readers do not behave strategically (see Paris & Lindauer, 1982). Paris, Lipson, and Wixson, for example, have argued that strategic readers are those who possess knowledge and control as well as a willingness to employ available resources in flexible ways to accomplish academic goals. They have suggested that children can only be truly strategic when they understand the when and why of the skills and strategies they possess.

A distinction must be made here between conscious, deliberate strategic acts and other, more routine processing that occurs. During reading, certain skills such as word analysis should be performed habitually or automatically. Automaticity is not an issue in whether one is or is not reading strategically. The choosing of relevant strategies are acts of metacognition which include some degree of monitoring, checking, and self-testing and the readers' capable decisions concerning the degree required. In this way, effective readers use metacognition in their efforts to become strategic readers.

It is encouraging that metacognition and strategic reading behavior seem to be related to instruction as well as to development. Attempts at teaching children the knowledge and control required to be more expert at reading have demonstrated that young children and poor readers can make significant progress when instruction is appropriate (Au & Mason, 1981; Hansen & Pearson, 1984; Palincsar & Brown, in press; Paris, Cross, & Lipson, 1984). The instructional program should move the student from dependence on the teacher to independence as a reader. To achieve this goal, teachers need to teach comprehension skills, model them in teaching, and give students opportunities to practice such techniques in situations outside the classroom and beyond the text. The teacher must then gradually help students to develop strategies that will work best for them as independent readers.

Skilled readers are flexible. How they read depends upon the complexity of the text, their familiarity with the topic, and their purpose for reading.
–Scott Paris

Instructional Framework for Developing Strategic Readers

A fundamental goal of reading comprehension instruction should be to teach students to become self-directed, strategic readers who analyze, plan, monitor, and regulate their reading behavior.

Strategic readers exercise control over their reading. To do this, they need to know about the topic, text, and task. They also need skills and to know how, why, and when to use them in a variety of situations. Finally, students' interests and attitudes play an important role in whether they will use knowledge and skills when reading. Figure 3 provides a framework for developing strategic behavior in the classroom. An explanation of that framework follows.

Knowledge

Strategic readers need knowledge about the topic of a selection to be able to make interpretations. Making interpretations is part of the inferencing process that is central to all comprehension. Readers connect ideas from what they know with information in the text to construct meaning. Knowledge about the topic is also a source for testing the *sense making* of the information presented in the text (Baker, Brown, 1984).

Readers also need to have knowledge about different kinds of texts, how the texts are organized, and how this organization can aid comprehension. A scope and sequence for instructing narrative and expository text structures is found in section 4. Finally, strategic readers need to have knowledge about reading tasks. This knowledge includes knowing the purpose for the reading, such as an assignment, personal interest, or information, and knowing the expected outcomes, such as a test, a discussion, or following directions.

Skills

Strategic readers need to have not only the skills of word analysis, comprehension, and problem solving, but also must know *how, when,* and *why* to use each skill. These skills and the knowledge about them accumulate as a result of instruction and experiences (Paris, Oka, DeBritto, 1983).

Students typically demonstrate how to use isolated skills on worksheets and criterion-referenced tests. However, the most crucial part is knowing how to put the skills to use as strategies while reading. For example, students who have been taught to use a consonant-vowel-consonant (CVC) pattern to pronounce words may do well on the workbook pages or pass a test in which the skill is tested, but learning the CVC pattern is not an end in itself. Rather, students should be guided to incorporate skills into a strategy for figuring out new words in context. Similarly, students may do well in an exercise selecting the main idea from three or four choices presented on a worksheet, but fail to find main ideas while reading on their own. Students need guidance to incorporate their skill knowledge about main ideas into strategies for locating main ideas while reading.

Beyond knowing how, strategic readers need to know why strategies are effective and when they should be applied. Students can become proficient enough with various strategies to do them on teacher command, but it takes several more conditions to get them to use the strategies independently; those conditions are knowing why and when and having the attitudes and interest to use them. For example, why and when is it useful to skim a selection for main ideas? Or why and when is it important to reread? Strategic readers need to know why strategies are effective and when they should be applied. Teachers in all subject areas can help students develop these skills by including why and when demonstrations as part of instruction.

The test of great teachers is whether they have helped their students to independence, to doing without them.
–Edgar Dale (1965)

Attitudes and Interests

Attitudes or interests reflect the motivated intent of a reader to comprehend a selection. Self-motivation depends on

Personal Significance of the Reading Task. How much does it mean to me? What interests do I have for completing this reading? What benefits do I get out of reading this?

Utility and Efficiency. What strategies should I use for the task? How easy and useful are these strategies?

Effort. How much time and energy do I have to put in for a positive result?

Students need to be persuaded of the importance of the reading task and of choosing appropriate strategies. Task goals selected by the teacher run the risk of being rejected since the reader may not see the personal significance. If students don't judge the strategy useful or if the strategy requires too much time or effort, it is unlikely they will use it on their own.

Instructional Framework for Developing Strategic Behavior

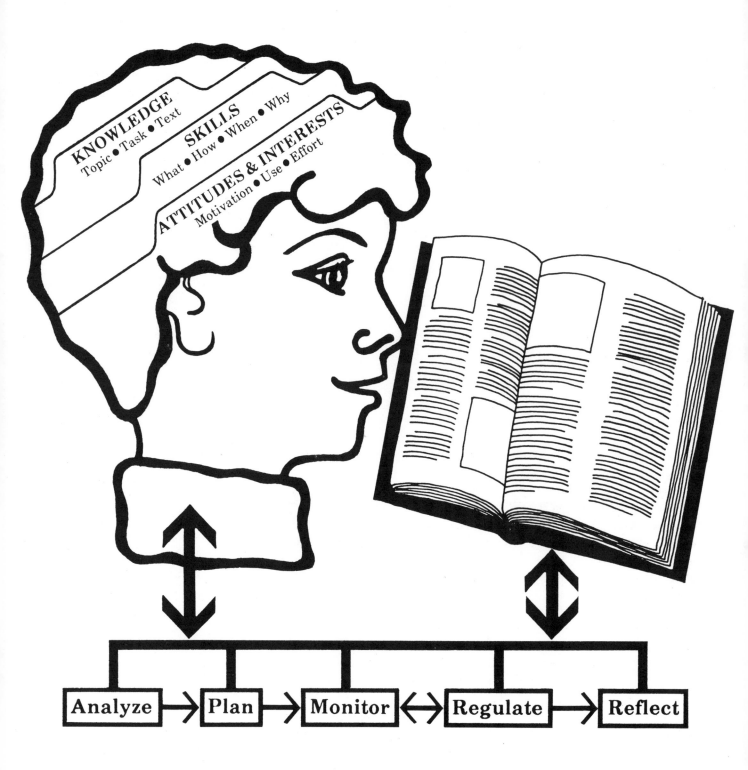

Strategic readers exercise control of their reading by *analyzing, planning, monitoring,* and *regulating* their reading, drawing upon whatever specific strategies they have in their repertoire to be effective comprehenders (Paris, Lipson, & Wixson, 1983). To analyze, readers examine the text features and the nature of the assignment to determine the purpose of the reading task. Planning involves selecting purposes and strategies for reading. When a reader consciously applies a reading skill to a particular reading task, the result is a strategy. The following list of skills should be taught as effective strategies for achieving a purpose. It is important to realize that the list is not all inclusive.

Reading is an interactive constructive and strategic process. Readers make sense of what they read by integrating text information with their own knowledge, by monitoring their understanding, and by using procedures for reinterpreting what they read.
–G. Duffy, L. Roehler (1984)

■ Table 2

Effective Strategies

- Previewing
- Self-questioning from the simplest level ("Do I understand?") to complicated self-study questioning
- Using context and grapho-phonemic clues for word pronunciation
- Using context and structural clues for word meanings
- Adjusting reading speed to difficulty of material
- Rereading
- Making predictions, confirming or rejecting the predictions, revising, and predicting again
- Placing the problem "on hold" and reading on for more information
- Comparing material to prior knowledge
- Going to another, perhaps easier text source
- Seeking information from outside sources
- Paraphrasing
- Looking for important ideas
- Suspending judgment
- Summarizing to integrate information
- Looking for relationships
- Skimming
- Scanning
- Taking notes

After readers have developed a plan, they begin to read, putting the strategies on automatic control while monitoring their comprehension. The basic monitoring question is, "Am I comprehending?" Readers' antennas are set to pick up or check for interference signals. When a problem is registered, readers leave the monitoring phase and move to regulation. They regulate by adjusting strategies and applying suitable additional strategies to fix or debug the problem.

Role of Teachers

Sharing knowledge about reading strategies during instruction helps students understand how and why they should use particular tactics.
–Lipson, Wixon

Teachers play a major role in helping students develop strategic reading behavior. As teachers plan instruction, they need to assess their students' knowledge about the topic, the text, the task, and the needed skills. They need to teach and model strategic behavior, showing students how to analyze, plan, monitor, and regulate their reading and then gradually move from the role of instructor to that of guide and coach encouraging students to independently analyze, plan, monitor, and regulate their reading. Teachers' guidance and coaching should be both explicit and supportive. The abilities to be a strategic reader are developed through repeated experiences with teachers who criticize, evaluate, and extend the limits of their students' experiences (Baker & Brown, 1984). Teachers might find it useful to evaluate their efforts by referring to figure 3 and addressing the following questions.

● Do I always activate students' background knowledge of the topic? the text structure? the reading task?

● Do I teach students what the skill can accomplish?

● Do I teach students how to integrate the skill into appropriate specific strategies?

● Do I demonstrate why the skill is useful and when it is appropriate to use it?

● Do I attend to students' attitude and interest factors?

● Do I guide students to incorporate specific strategies into a global strategy whenever they analyze, plan, monitor, and regulate their own comprehension?

● Do I praise and support readers who are trying to use strategies independently?

Assessing Strategic Reading Behavior

Strategic reading requires student time and effort to analyze reading goals, plan available actions, monitor comprehension, and regulate or adjust the strategies as needed. To assess how well students are doing, teachers need to model and talk about strategies used and why, and then encourage students to share their knowledge of strategic behavior. The research by Paris, Lipson and Wixson (1983) refers to this as "reading becoming public" or "thinking out loud."

Engaging students in small group discussions about their reading or conducting one or more interviews can provide the teacher with valuable clues to strategic behavior. Teachers might use the following questions with their students.

Analysis

- What is the first thing you do when you begin reading?
- What is the hardest part about reading for you?
- What would help you become a better reader?
- Is there anything special about the first sentence or two? What do they tell you?
- How about the last sentence; what does it tell you?
- How can you tell which sentences are the most important ones?

Planning

- Before you start to read, do you do anything special? What kinds of plans help you read better?
- If you would only read some sentences because you were in a hurry, which ones would you read?
- What would you try to tell someone about what you read? All the words? Just the ending? What it was about? Or something else?
- If you had to remember what you read for future use, what would you do? Underline? Take notes?

Monitoring and Regulation

- Do you ever go back and read things over? Why?
- What do you do if you come to a word you don't understand?
- What do you do if you don't understand a whole sentence?
- What parts do you skip as you read?
- What things do you read faster than others?

Teachers also need to monitor and observe strategic behaviors during reading class (see model in Appendix A). The following description is an example of what teachers might look for as students demonstrate strategic behavior.

Strategic Reading: Reading Class

In a recent reading class, the teacher introduced Scott's reading group to an African folktale called "All Stories are Anansi's." Prior to reading, the group reviewed the basic components of story structure and talked about how to use this knowledge to help understand and recall the story. They talked about tricks they had played and tried to predict what Anansi, the trickster, would do in the story.

When Scott got to his desk, he paged through the story to check its length and looked at the illustration to see if the story was going to be "a good one." His analysis revealed the story might be interesting because "there are some very humorous pictures." However, he thought it might be difficult to follow and remember because it was the longest folktale the students had read so far. Scott planned his strategy for reading. At each new point in the story, he would review what he had read and predict what was going to happen next.

As he monitored his understanding, Scott became increasingly sure of himself—he passed each checkpoint easily. Only once did he run into a snag. That's when he came to the word "calabash." Since Anansi seemed to be using a calabash to play a trick, he decided he needed to figure out the meaning. To fix or regulate the problem, he applied phonics analysis and succeeded in getting the pronunciation. Then he reread the sentence in which "calabash" first appeared, learning from context clues that a "calabash" is a big jug or pot that holds water. Scott used his knowledge of story structure to help him remember the important information from the story. Through discussion the teacher could see that Scott was using strategic behavior to comprehend.

K-12 Scope and Sequence: Skills and Strategies 4

Introduction
Word Meaning
Word Analysis
Text Organization
Critical Reading and Thinking
Responding in Writing
Attitudes and Interests

Introduction

Students of all ages would benefit from a renewed instructional focus on the more complex comprehension skills and strategies.
–Reading Report Card (1985)

Underlying the framework found in this section of the guide is the understanding that reading comprehension involves a merging of reader, text, and context that goes far beyond merely processing the meaning of a string of decoded words and that reading comprehension is greater than the sum of its parts. To get meaning or gain information from a given text, readers use different skills and strategies necessary for comprehending or remembering. The skills and strategies, highlighted within the framework, are components of an effective reading program and need to be emphasized in K-12 instruction. Each component is described in this section with a consideration of *why* the component is important, *what* it involves, and *how* it can be taught and its effectiveness measured. Scope and sequence charts are included for each component. Each of these components should be considered within the framework for the development of strategic behavior which was described in the preceding section.

Word Meaning

Why Is Word Meaning Important?

Word meaning is a necessary yet limited factor in reading comprehension. A strong meaning vocabulary is necessary for comprehending text. However, it does not insure comprehension. In order for comprehension to occur, the reader must analyze the words, recognize the interrelationships among them, and derive meaning from the unique combinations used by authors. Word meaning represents a strong underlying conceptual network of knowledge that supports reading comprehension.

What Should Be Considered In Teaching Vocabulary?

First, the goal of reading instruction is comprehension; vocabulary growth is of value only as it serves to further reading comprehension. A reader can read a selection not knowing the meaning of every word and yet comprehend the selection if such words are not crucial to the information and ideas in the selection. Second, incidental learning through everyday experiences accounts for a substantial amount of vocabulary knowledge. Third, words are learned and retained when used frequently in reading, writing, and speaking and when connections are made between the new words and prior knowledge. Fourth, the greater the prior knowledge students have of the meanings of related words under study, the easier the new words are to learn and retain over the long term.

Prior knowledge makes such a strong impact on learning that it is important to describe some of its patterns.

Oral/Aural Vocabulary. These are words in the students' speaking/listening vocabulary that they cannot yet read. Once students can decode these words they usually know their meanings. The knowledge possessed by Emergent and Beginning Readers is based primarily on experiences from natural language settings. The language experience approach uses the natural language as the basis for beginning reading instruction. Commercial publishers of beginning reading materials also attempt to choose words familiar to students.

Meaning is constructed as readers link what they read to what they know.

New Word Labels for Known Meanings. These words are also referred to as synonyms. The student may know the meaning of a word such as car and then learn a new label, automobile, for the same meaning. This experience is common to Emergent, Beginning Reading and Reading for Consolidation stages.

New Meanings for Known Words. Referred to as multiple meaning words, these words are already known to students. However, the meaning is for one situation and needs to be expanded to include meanings for other contexts. Multiple meaning words are particularly problematic in content-area reading where a familiar word suddenly assumes a different meaning. Therefore, these words should receive particular emphasis beginning with the Reading for Consolidation stage.

New Words, Easily Learned. These words are not in students' oral nor reading vocabulary. Students do not know their meanings, but meanings can easily be built because students have related background knowledge which can be used in instruction to connect the known with the unknown.

New Words, Difficult to Learn. These words also are not in students' oral nor reading vocabulary. Students don't know meanings, and because they have limited or no background knowledge on the topic, they have difficulty developing meanings.

As students progress into the Reading for Consolidation and the stages that follow, they read more about new topics with specialized vocabulary and complex concepts. As a result more new words fall in the new words, easily learned, and difficult to learn categories.

How Can Teachers Help Students To Acquire New Vocabulary?

The following categories of words are not mutually exclusive. Often a word can fall into several categories depending on its use in a given text. However, this categorization is useful in focusing attention on the function of words in text.

High frequency words occur so often in print that they are essential to fluent reading, particularly in the beginning stages. These words need to be recognized at sight.

Text - critical words are absolutely necessary to understand a particular selection. Technical vocabulary and words representing specific concepts are included in this category.

Structural words consist of root words and prefixes or suffixes, which change the meanings of the words.

General vocabulary includes the remaining words in a text not specified by the above, including synonyms, antonyms, homographs, and homophones.

Each of these categories is important at each of the development stages. However, the degree of emphasis may differ. During Emergent and Beginning Reading stages, students learn the high frequency words so that both pronunciation and meaning become automatic. Technical vocabulary, a subset of text critical words, becomes a more direct concern beginning with the Reading for Consolidation stage. It is at this stage in elementary schools that most students acquire textbooks in several different fields.

How Should Words Be Selected?

Upon preview of the reading selection, the teacher should select those words that are necessary for comprehension and then determine how well the students need to know the words. The gist of the meaning may be sufficient, or a fully developed conceptual meaning may be necessary. The following recommendations suggest ways to proceed.
● Teach words central to the important ideas in the selection.
● Teach only the words students do not already know.
● Expect students to develop meaning during reading if there is a good context.
● Teach a few words well (five or less) so that students retain them over a long term.

Before instruction begins, the classroom teacher needs to determine the extent of students' vocabulary knowledge, more specifically their knowledge of words related to the topics under study. The following informal procedures are easiest to employ.
● Observe oral language usage during discussions and listen for students' knowledge of words and meanings central to the topic.
● Pretest the key terms that will appear in a new unit of instruction.
● Encourage the students to tell what they already know about the concept.
● Ask the question, "What can you tell me about this word?", instead of requiring its use in a sentence.

. . . attempts to improve comprehension are more likely to be productive if consideration is given to the components of the comprehension process and the abilities and knowledge required to perform these processes and the instructional procedures used to promote the abilities and teach the knowledge.
–Isabel Beck (1983)

How Can Teachers Help Students Acquire Strategies for Developing Word Meanings?

Throughout instruction teachers need to encourage students to develop strategies for determining word meanings. It is the teachers' role to consistently guide students to use available clues to develop word meanings on their own and, thus, move toward independence as readers. Instruction should guide students to

- read a paragraph, perhaps a single sentence;
- ask themselves if they understand what they read;
- determine which specific words hinder understanding;
- consider how to develop meanings for problem words;
- look for possible clues to meaning in surrounding text;
- think of who might be asked for help in developing meanings.

It is important to stress that students be guided to develop strategies for figuring out meanings themselves. Students might find it helpful to use the sample bookmark included below. A sample poster for guiding independent use of strategies is included in Appendix B.

✧ Does it make sense? If not,
✧ What word don't I know?
✧ How can I find out?
✧ What clues? Who can help?

Teachers should model first the use of context clues, then other strategies when the surrounding text is not helpful. The use of a dictionary should be encouraged for students at Reading to Learn the New stage and beyond. Dictionaries are ineffective with young children since definitions are often far removed from their experiences.

How Can Word Meaning Learning Be Assessed?

Follow-up assessment may include observations to identify students' use of new vocabulary words in speaking and writing activities. Teachers may use paper and pencil tests, keeping in mind that students may believe they have to remember meanings only until tested. For this reason, it is important to incorporate newly acquired vocabulary into daily instructional activities.

Summary

Strategic readers independently monitor word meaning in a given text. They know when they don't know the meaning of a word and when it interferes with comprehension. They know if it is necessary to work to develop the meaning, and they select strategies for finding out the meaning which include the following.

- Reading another simpler book about the topic
- Rereading the surrounding text
- Talking it over with another student or the teacher
- Seeking out any number of other experiences that will help develop the concept

Word Meaning

Stage	Teacher	Student
Emergent Reading	Reads stories aloud	Listens and develops listening vocabulary
	Provides opportunities for story-telling and retelling Discusses new words and relates them to prior knowledge	Uses new words in oral context
Beginning Reading	Reads stories aloud	Listens and develops listening vocabulary
	Teaches high frequency words	Begins to use high frequency words automatically
	Teaches selected new words in preparation for reading – critical words from text – general vocabulary	Uses word meaning to comprehend story Uses new words to write questions and responses Uses new words to write stories Uses new words in a variety of contexts
	Teaches common prefixes	Uses prefix knowledge to assist in identifying word meaning in context
	Guides development of semantic maps for new topics under study	Orally relates new topic to known words and word meanings
Reading for Consolidation	Reads stories aloud	Listens and develops listening vocabulary
	Teaches selected new words in preparation for selections from readers and textbooks – critical words from text – general vocabulary – technical vocabulary	Uses word meanings to comprehend Uses new words to write responses to questions Uses new words to write reports and stories Uses new words in a variety of contexts
	Teaches more difficult prefixes	Uses prefix knowledge to assist in identification of word meaning in context
	Guides development of semantic maps for new topics under study	Relates new topic to known words and word meanings

Word Meaning *(continued)*

Stage	Teacher	Student
Reading for Consolidation *(continued)*	Guides development of semantic maps for new topics under study	Compares words that are roughly synonymous to determine subtle differences in meanings in relationship to the topic
Reading to Learn the New	Begins to guide students toward independence in learning word meanings	Begins to identify unknown words and develops a strategy for learning new words independently (beyond mere dictionary use)
	Teaches common Greek and Latin roots functionally	Uses Greek and Latin roots to identify word meaning in context
	Guides students to use the dictionary for studying	Relates dictionary definition to prior experience and context
Reading for Independence	Organizes vocabulary instruction according to interdisciplinary concepts and processes	Recognizes different terminology for similar concepts and processes among the content
	Helps students to identify and enlarge their word meaning strategies	Applies a variety of word meaning strategies during the entire reading process (pre-, during, and post reading)
	Guides students to use the dictionary for research	Applies all components of the dictionary to gather data on selected topics and to solve problems
Mature Reading	Models how to define words related to use	Adjusts strategies for defining words in both oral and written language
	Models how to evaluate the appropriateness of an author's choice of words	Assesses author's word choice
	Models a variety of other methods for expanding vocabulary growth	Develops a personal system for enriching vocabulary
	Guides students to compare and contrast dictionaries	Identifies the strengths and weaknesses of dictionaries for stated purposes

Why Is Word Analysis Important?

Word analysis is a strategy used to help decode unfamiliar words. The term word analysis is frequently used interchangeably with other labels such as decoding, word identification, word attack, and word recognition and is a part of the overall reading comprehension development. Although its main focus is in the beginning reading stages, the strategy remains with the reader throughout successive stages as more advanced, technical, and foreign words are encountered in text materials. It is important that a reader of limited vocabulary, at any age or grade level, understand that the processes for analyzing words and developing meaning are mutually supportive.

The main purpose of providing instruction in word analysis skills is to help students gain ability to independently construct meaning from print. This involves instructing students to recognize known words as described in the previous section and to develop meaning from unfamiliar words.

What Word Analysis Skills Should Be Taught?

Word analysis skills to be taught will vary according to basic reading programs adopted by schools. However, recent research provides some general direction on how instruction should proceed.

Some students will need detailed instruction in word analysis, while others may learn to apply strategies independently with very little assistance The optimum amount of instruction is the minimum amount required to help each student become independent in developing meaning from unfamiliar words.

Two kinds of clues are available to assist students in identifying an unknown word. First is its context, which consists of the syntax of the sentence and the semantics of words in the written passage. Both syntax and semantics serve to limit possibilities for the word's meaning in that use. Only certain meanings will make sense in the overall textual content.

Second are the clues offered by parts of the unfamiliar word itself. These clues can be structural or phonic. Some amount of structural and phonic knowledge is useful to the developing reader. Phonics is a means to an end and should never be emphasized at the expense of meaning. A useful guide as to what phonic skills should be included in a reading curriculum is found in table 3.

Phonics instruction should go hand in hand with opportunities to identify words in meaningful sentences and stories.
–Becoming a Nation of Readers

35

Phonics: What Should Be Taught

Major Letter-Sound Correspondence

For each pattern sample words are used to illustrate the letter-sound relationships that need to be learned. Occasionally a rule is given.

Consonants

b – book	j – job	n – new	s – sit or was	x – xylophone
d – dance	k – king	p – party	t – top or nation	exam, tax
f – funny	l – lemon	qu – queen	v – violin	y – yes
h – heart	m – money	r – roll	w – water	z – zebra

Other Consonants

c – cent – city – cycle
c – cat – cot – cup

Rule: C sounds likes s before e, i, y, and sounds like k elsewhere.

g – gem/agile/gym
g – game/gone/guild

Rule: G sounds like j before e, i, y, and sounds like g elsewhere.

Double Consonants

diagraphs	doubles	
ch – chew/choir/chef	bb – rabble	nn – funny
ph – photo	cc – buccaneer/accept	mm – dimmer
th – thin/this	dd – ladder	pp – happen
wh – while	ff – jiffy	rr – narrow
ng – song	gg – egg/suggest	vv – savvy
sh – shoe	ll – belly	zz – dizzy

Rule: Except for cc and gg, two identical consonants have one sound.

Blends

bl – black	br – brown	sc – scat	sp – spot
cl – clue	cr – cry	scr – screen	squ – squeak
fl – flap	dr – draw	sm – small	st – stump
gl – glass	fr – friend	sn – snow	sw – swing
pl – play	gr – ground		
sl – slow	pr – proud		
	tr – trap		

Silent Letters kn – knee   wr – wrong   mb – comb   ten – fasten

Vowels

i – if	a – act	o – hot	e – bed	u – much
mild	about	of	jacket	cute
bird	ape	note	blaze	tube
	want	off	often	bull
	call	for	she	fur
	star		her	

Rules:
1. A vowel between two consonants is usually short: pin, cap, hot, bug, bed.
2. A vowel before two or more consonants is usually short: wish, graph, much, blotter, lettuce, happen, itch, hospital, cinder, bumper.
3. A vowel followed by a consonant plus e is usually long: pine, date, dope, cute, mete.
4. The letter y sometimes is a vowel and it has two sounds: my, baby.

Double Vowels

io – nation	ou – ounce	au – because	ai – pain	ee – see
lion	though	laugh	said	been
ea – teach	soup	oo – moon	ay – play	oi – coin
bread	would	book		ow – own
great				cow

Adapted from Johnson, D.; Pearson, P.D., Teaching Reading Vocabulary, 1984.

A major problem with current reading instruction is that phonic and other word analysis skills are taught in isolation. Too often teachers consider instruction effective if students are able to fill in blanks on worksheets or in workbooks. The true test of teaching effectiveness is the students' ability to use various word analysis strategies when reading independently. The successful teacher guides readers through effective skills-selection processes, encourages use of all clues, and avoids wasting the students' time with superfluous skill reinforcement or testing. Following instruction students should have many opportunities to practice their skills with meaningful reading materials. Most of the basic instruction in word analysis skills should be completed by the end of the Beginning Reading stage as suggested by the scope and sequence at the end of this section.

...Do it early. Keep it simple. Except in cases of diagnosed individual need, phonics instruction should have been completed by the end of the second grade.
–Becoming a Nation of Readers

How Should Word Analysis Be Taught?

Comprehension depends a great deal on rapid as well as accurate word recognition. Students who labor over word pronunciation will have difficulty understanding whole messages, just as bicycle riders who steer and pedal capably but too slowly will tip over rather than cover much ground. Instruction should develop word recognition skills to the point where they are automatic, accurate, and rapid. The development from slow, deliberate reading to fluent and ultimately independent reading involves what has been termed *automaticity* (Laberge and Samuels, 1977). To help students gain fluency as they automate (make habitual) the specific underlying skills involved (Perfetti, 1977), teachers should teach decoding skills within the context of meaningful passages of text.

■ Figure 4

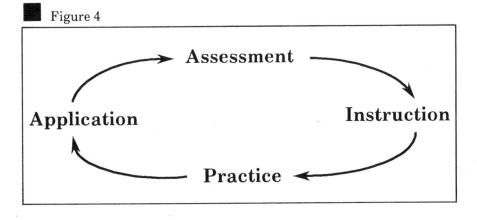

How and When Should Word Analysis Skills Be Assessed?

Instruction should always be guided by what individual students need to help them identify unfamiliar words. Preassessment is, therefore, essential to identify which skills are known and which are unknown to the readers. Word analysis teaching is a continuous cyclical process as illustrated in figure 4.

A more detailed plan for making teaching decisions about word analysis instruction appears in Appendix C.

Through constant practice in reading different kinds of text, students will develop independence in using appropriate word analysis strategies. Since this independence should be the guiding principle for teachers at all levels, there must be an ongoing assessment of how students apply strategies in reading. At all stages, teacher judgment becomes the most valuable method of evaluation. Listening to students read aloud provides useful clues to word analysis strategies as well as to understanding of content. Competency in applying strategies can be measured by the students' ability to transfer practice skills to reading textual passages.

It is through reading that we develop the skill that enables us to identify unfamiliar words, words not in our sight vocabulary.
—James Moffett

Summary

Using word analysis strategies helps students determine the meaning of unfamiliar words and enables them to become independent readers. They should be encouraged to form predictions and to use what they do know to figure out what a word might be. A strategic reader habitually decides whether phonics, context clues, or a combination of clues is needed to identify unfamiliar words. Teachers should always strive to develop that independence in students.

Word Analysis

Stage	Teacher	Student
Emergent Reading	Reads stories aloud	Listens and becomes aware of language patterns
	Pronounces familiar words	Listens and identifies rhyming elements of words and phrases
	Guides recognition of environmental print	Recognizes environmental signs and symbols (stop signs and cereal boxes)
	Discusses letters of alphabet	Matches and names upper and lower case letters Begins to develop sound-letter correspondence
Beginning Reading	Reads stories aloud	Listens and becomes aware of language patterns and word meanings
	Teaches integration of phonics, structural, and contextual analysis	Associates sounds with letters in words for beginning and ending consonants
	Models *what*, *how*, *when*, and *why* for each skill	Associates sounds with letters in words for blends and digraphs
	Provides guided practice	Associates sounds with letters in words for long and short vowels
	Provides appropriate independent practice	Recognizes parts of words: roots, prefixes, and suffixes Recognizes elements of compound words Recognizes and understands function of contractions, plurals, and possessive forms Identifies words by use in sentences Uses integrated strategies to pronounce unfamiliar words in context
	Teaches and guides independence in use of word analysis strategy in oral and written context	Begins to apply decoding skills flexibly
	Provides independent reading time	Applies and internalizes word analysis concepts Reads for meaning and comprehension

Word Analysis *(continued)*

Stage	Teacher	Student
Reading for Consolidation	Guides and facilitates as needed	Applies word analysis strategies to acquire reading independence (automaticity)
Reading to Learn the New	Guides and facilitates as needed	Utilizes word analysis strategies with a variety of materials (as necessary) Applies word analysis for word meaning to acquire reading independence
Reading from Independence	Guides and facilitates as needed	Utilizes word analysis strategies with a variety of materials (if necessary)
Mature Reading	Guides and facilitates as needed	Utilizes word analysis strategies in personal and career situations

Text organization refers to the system of arranging ideas in text and the nature of the relationships among those ideas. Sometimes referred to as the text structure, it is the pattern chosen as the means for best expressing the writer's ideas. Knowledge of text structure allows the reader to identify the hierarchy of the writers ideas and consequently to get to the most important points of a passage. The ability of the reader to recognize and use text structure significantly improves comprehension (Meyer, 1975, Stein, 1978). Older readers show more awareness of text structure than do younger readers; skilled readers make more effective use of structure than poorer readers.

Until recently publishers and educators perceived comprehension in terms of a taxonomy including literal, inferential, and evaluative questions and answers. However, when questions are formulated from a taxonomy and with little regard for the basic structure of the text, there is a tendency toward fragmented comprehension. In contrast, lessons organized around the textual structure help students to see the text as a whole, perceiving the relationships among the various parts of the text. In recent years, researchers have developed systems to describe the structure of both narrative and expository texts. These systems are described below.

There appears to be a growing realization that the emphasis on basic skills has had a negative impact on students' abilities to actively interact with and critically evaluate written text.
—John Goodlad (1983)

Narrative Text

Why is Knowledge of Narrative Text Organization Helpful?

If students have a knowledge of the parts of the story and the sequence in which these events are arranged, they are better able to organize the oncoming information and focus on the most important parts they read. Also, they can use their knowledge of story structure as a way of remembering the story and organizing their summaries.

What Should Be Included in Narrative Text Instruction?

Story structure or story grammar is a vehicle for comprehending story content as a cohesive unit rather than as a series of unrelated details. Study of structure has resulted in detailed diagrams that illustrate relationships among story parts. These diagrams are like outlines or maps analagous to the structure of the skyscraper that defines the basic shape of a building and all its parts. A simplified listing of basic components of most narrative stories and novels appears below. An example of a story map for a familiar folk tale, "The Three Billy Goats Gruff," is included in Appendix D.

Setting: where and when the story happened.

Characters: major and minor individuals involved.

Problem: the conflict the main character or characters try to resolve.

Goal: what the main character(s) hopes to achieve by solving the problem.

Plot: series of related episodes usually including introductory event(s), a development (or main action), and a resolution.

Resolution: the conclusion (outcome) of character(s) in relation to the problem and goal.

How Should Narrative Organization Be Taught?

The major purpose of developing a story map is to identify the central structure and content of a story in order to recall the important parts and thus be able to think critically about the reading.

The structure of narrative stories becomes increasingly complex and varied as students are exposed to various literary forms throughout their school years. The fable can initially be described with a simple story map which may then be expanded and modified to reflect more complex variations in story structure. For example, there might be a main character with multiple problems and goals, several main characters with various problems and goals, episodes embedded within episodes, a time sequence that includes flashbacks, and missing plot events that must be inferred by the readers.

The scope and sequence suggested on pages 44-45 represents a general sequence, not necessarily a hierarchical one. A major developmental difference among reading stages is that awareness of story structure at earlier stages is typically intuitive and not thoroughly formulated. As knowledge becomes conscious, students are able to use structure intentionally for specific purposes. However, at any stage, students may participate in a wide range of simple-to-complex structure-based activities involving the organization of narrative reading material.

How Can Understanding of Narrative Text Be Assessed?

A structure is always present when students read stories (narratives) so the challenge for the teacher is to guide their use of the structure to assist comprehension. Teachers can have students retell a story and observe if all the important parts are included. They can devise written or oral questions to see which parts of the story are understood and remembered. Not to be overlooked is careful observation of the discussion of stories to see if students are using their knowledge of structure to help them comprehend.

Summary

Story structure defines the central organization and content of narrative stories or novels. Readers can use it to understand and recall concepts and extend their comprehension through critical analysis and evaluation of literature. Teachers can use it successfully to teach comprehension more efficiently and effectively.

Narrative Text

Stage	Teacher	Student
Emergent Reading	Reads stories aloud	Listens and develops sense of stories
	Introduces story map terminology	Incorporates story map terminology into listening vocabulary
	Uses wordless picture books to develop concept of story	Tells story in own words, incorporating major story parts
Beginning Reading	Reads stories aloud	Listens and refines sense of stories Discriminates between stories which follow a map and those that don't
	Instructs in story map terminology	Uses terminology in speaking vocabulary
	Asks comprehension questions based on story structure	Begins to internalize and apply structure to enhance comprehension of simple and increasingly complex stories
	Incorporates language experience with story structure. Instructs on writing various parts of story map	Dictates story using story structure model. Writes variations on story map parts
	Develops writing lessons based on story structure using several episodes	Writes stories containing several episodes Engages in simple peer editing
Reading For Consolidation	Reads stories aloud	Listens and compares stories' similarities and differences
	Presents stories with multiple goals and problems	Identifies multiple goals and problems in stories during discussion
	Instructs in comparison of characters among stories	Makes comparisons from story to story based on story structure model
	Presents various literary forms and instructs in identification of each	Identifies and interprets different story forms
	Emphasizes story map structure and expects discussion on important parts	Internalizes story map elements and develops conscious awareness of these during reading
	Reinforces and models writing of basic story structure	Writes original stories, using basic structure

Stage	Teacher	Student
Reading for Consolidation *(continued)*	Reinforces and models writing of basic story structure	Analyzes and edits own and other readers' stories according to story map model
Reading to Learn the New	Continues to present various literary forms and instructs in interpretation of them	Refines identification and interpretation of different story forms
	Continues to emphasize story structure and expects use during discussions	Internalizes story structure and consciously uses it to organize, recall, and make inferences about the story Analyzes and edits own and other readers' stories according to different story forms
Reading for Independence	Continues to present various literary forms and instruct in their interpretation	Refines interpretation of different literary forms
	Continues to emphasize story structure and expects use during discussions	Has internalized story structure and consciously uses it to organize recall inferences about the story
	Instructs in refinement of several literary forms	Refines writing different literary forms Analyzes and edits own and other readers' stories according to different literary forms
	Guides students to compare and contrast different genres on the same theme	Evaluates the strengths and weaknesses of various forms of literature for a given theme
	Guides students to perceive a piece of literature from various perspectives	Role-plays various practitioners or personalities when interpreting a piece of literature
Mature Reading	Continues guidance in use of various literary forms for discussing and writing	Continues refinement of use of literary forms for thinking and writing
	Guides students to form their own generalizations about various genres	Applies various strategies for initiating and sustaining a satisfying reading momentum
	Helps students establish integrity in their own evaluation of literature	Articulates author's ideas while remaining open to new insights/ perspectives

Expository Text

Why Is Knowledge of Expository Text Helpful?

Both elementary and secondary students have a good deal of trouble understanding and using the structure of expository text. This is perhaps because in early grades they have encountered very little of this kind of text in their reading. Basals traditionally have concentrated on narrative text although in recent years there has been a trend away from presenting solely narrative material. Additionally, elementary content-area texts, which should be a source of exposure to expository writing, often use a pseudo-narrative form or story form to convey information.

As students move from reading narrative text to expository materials in subject areas, they need to learn to read more for information than to receive imaginatively arranged concepts. Use of expository structure, like narrative, helps students organize and integrate oncoming information, identify major points, recall information, and summarize. Students need to be instructed in the various text structures and appropriate strategies for comprehending and remembering text information. If expository text is well organized, students will find it easier to understand and remember the content. If the text is poorly organized, students will need to know how to adjust their strategies.

What Is Expository Text and How Is it Organized?

Expository text refers to textbooks, reference books, non-fiction books, pamphlets, and articles in all subject areas. Understanding and remembering main points from such sources are crucial for learning facts and concepts. Of special concern is how the author presents main ideas and supportive details. Readers need to determine if there is a pattern for organizing the main idea and whether main ideas are stated explicitly or implicitly. Main idea instruction is closely intertwined with the particular structure of the text and usually precedes any instruction on specific patterns.

The organization or structure of expository materials will vary within and across subject areas. Readers cannot expect textbooks to fall conveniently into one category. Both teachers and readers must know the text. Commonly occurring organizational patterns in expository writing have the following primary characteristics.

Description or Simple Listing: a listing of items or ideas where the order of presentation is not significant.

Temporal Sequence: a sequential relationship between ideas or events considered in terms of the passage of time.

Definition and Example: a definition of a key word or concept followed by an example.

Comparison and Contrast: a description of similarities and differences between two or more things.

Cause and Effect: interaction between at least two ideas or events, one considered a cause or reason and the other an effect or result.

Problem and Solution: similar to cause and effect pattern in that two factors interact, one citing a problem and the other a solution to that problem.

How Should Expository Text Be Taught?

The more thoroughly teachers prepare students to identify the organization of any text, the more likely students are to achieve comprehension in a given reading situation. Instead of simply assigning a chapter to be read, followed by discussion, teachers should help students examine organizational aids such as headings and subheadings, activate prior knowledge, and develop predictions about the content.

Student writing is one way of approaching the teaching of text structure. In primary grades students should be given the opportunity to write stories that use the various patterns. For example, children could compare and contrast a dog and a cat, describe a pet bird, list the steps in a cooking activity, or rewrite an informational article using a specific pattern. As students progress, the teacher can draw attention to the patterns used in their stories or have them rewrite an article using a specific pattern.

Research has shown that learning from expository text is affected by how clearly the structure is indicated in the text. In some texts, the structure is heavily signalled by the writers. Signalling includes explicit statements about the structure, introductory summary statements, and textual cues such as underlining, italics, and bold face. Students, especially those average or below average in reading abilities, seem to remember more from text that contains signalling. Teachers should instruct students in how to use these cues as an aid to studying and learning new material. Instructional activities should guide students to independently choose appropriate reading strategies based upon the nature and the purpose of a given text.

Reading instruction should meet the challenge of building from the knowledge that children bring to the school experience, by offering the richest texts that they are able to understand.
–Becoming a Nation of Readers

How Can Knowlege of Expository Text Be Assessed?

Teacher observations and guided discussions are the most efficient ways to assess how students use expository text organization to aid comprehension. Metacognitive assessments of text arrangement should occur as students independently develop strategies for reading and learning from expository text. Students can work on their own or in small groups to answer questions such as the following.
- What text features helped me find main ideas?
- What text features helped me recognize how main ideas are organized?
- What text features helped me verify my understanding?

● What study strategies helped me remember important information?

Writing is another way to demonstrate comprehension of the text (see Responding in Writing, pages 60-62).

Summary

Students moving from reading narrative to expository texts in different subject areas will need to recognize the organizational structure and features of expository writing. To understand new information and ideas in such texts, students must be able to organize content in their own minds and relate it to what they already know. Students should be taught common organization patterns and methods of using these as comprehension aids along with strategies for studying and remembering. Where expository text organization is unclear or illogical, strategic readers recognize that and change their strategies accordingly. Strategic readers have the ability to tailor their strategies to the demands of the reading situation.

Expository Text

Stage	Teacher	Student
Emergent Reading	Encourages students to share information about topics	Contributes information about a familiar topic
	Reads informational books aloud	Listens and asks questions
	Encourages predicting with illustrations and titles	Suggests predictions
	Guides children to retell an informational book	Retells informational book
Beginning Reading	Assesses students' background knowledge about informational books and encourages students to categorize information	Shares experiences and information Notes differences in story and informational books
	Reads informational books and provides informational books for students to read	Listens, reads, and asks questions
	Encourages predicting after reading a few passages aloud	States predictions and listens to verify predictions
	Assesses students' knowledge of a topic Guides discussions of experience charts Demonstrates structure through experience charts	Shares ideas and experiences, dictates information for experience charts, and writes experience charts
	Guides students to reflect about an informational book	Contributes to group discussion about information contained in book
Reading For Consolidation	Activates background knowledge about a topic	Contributes ideas and categorizes information about a topic
	Guides students to preview selection for type of information and its organization Organizes instruction for accomplishment of reading process and content-area objectives	Participates in previewing reading selections for type of information and organization
	Teaches students to brainstorm, predict, and check understanding of factual content while reading	Monitors own comprehension by putting ideas from reading into own words and noting relationships of ideas in text

Expository Text *(continued)*

Stage	Teacher	Student
Reading for Consolidation *(continued)*	Models setting purpose for reading	Cooperatively sets purpose for reading expository text
	Guides students to identify main ideas and supporting details (explicit and implicit)	Locates main ideas and support ing details
	Models summarizing the major ideas of simple text	Summarizes the major ideas of simple text
	Models and encourages expository writing	Experiments with different ways to write expository information
Reading to Learn the New	Continues to organize instruction for process and content objectives	Previews text, sets purpose, and assesses task
	Guides students to set purpose and activate prior knowledge	Applies background knowledge to predict
	Models and guides developing semantic maps for organizing main ideas	Organizes main ideas into semantic map
	Helps students see relationships among sentences and paragraphs and models note-taking strategies	Uses note-taking strategies for studying
	Models and instructs summarizing of complex text by deleting trivial and repetitious materials (see Appendix E)	Summarizes text by deleting trivial and repetitious material and writes brief summaries
	Models writing brief summaries	
Reading for Independence	Continues to organize process and and content objective	Analyzes task and sets purpose
	Guides students to analyze materials using text structure	Uses text structure as a strategy for analysis
	Guides students to compare and contrast different text structures	Compares different text structures
	Helps students to see how to impose structure when it is not there	Imposes structures on text when lacking or implied

Stage	Teacher	Student
Reading for Independence *(continued)*	Guides and models analyzing task and setting purpose	Analyzes task and sets purpose
	Models note-taking strategies with a variety of materials and lecture	Uses note-taking strategies with a variety of materials and lecture
	Models and guides students to develop strategies for studying and learning from text, including use of signals to identify text structure and development of questions or a study guide	Analyzes task and text, and plans appropriate strategies for studying and learning from text Develops questions (study guide) for reading and studying
	Models and instructs summarizing by substituting a general term for specific items, combining a list of actions to broader category, and selecting a topic sentence	Summarizes text by substituting a general term for specific items, combining lists of actions, and selecting topic sentence to show comprehension of text
	Instructs when and where to use summarizing	Chooses appropriate task for summarizing
	Helps students develop reference skills for gaining information from a variety of materials	Uses text organization to skim and scan for reference
	Guides students to use the library and other sources for gaining and organizing additional information	Makes generalizations about where to locate expository materials and locates additional information about a topic
Mature Reading	Provides opportunities for utilizing text structure for reviewing text and task, sets purpose, and determines appropriate strategies	Independently applies text structure knowledge to a wide range of materials
	Expects students to accommodate a wide variety of expository materials	Analyzes text and task, sets purpose, and plans appropriate strategies
	Models and instructs summarizing by paraphrasing and writing summaries from complex material	Summarizes text from complex material

Critical Reading and Thinking

Why Are Critical Reading and Thinking Skills Important?

Although critical thinking is an essential component of reading comprehension, recent reports from the National Assessment of Educational Progress indicate that students today possess "very few skills for examining the nature of ideas that they take away from reading." That is to say, young people are not able to analyze and evaluate text materal; they are likely to be merely passive receptors.

Critical reading and thinking are necessary for citizens of a democratic and highly sophisticated technological society. Decisions required of the citizen, consumer, and worker all call for thoughtful reflection. Indeed, one cannot function as an informed voter, a careful consumer, or a rational decision maker without engaging in critical reading and thinking.

What Is Meant by Critical Reading and Thinking Skills?

Critical readers are conscious of the power of printed messages. They realize that writers vary in their ability to present their ideas effectively and in the quality of information presented. Consequently, critical readers use analytical and evaluative skills of their own to think about what they read.

Three main factors influence the ability to read and think critically.

Knowledge and Experience. Critical readers must have appropriate background knowledge in order to make an informed judgement concerning a text. Without relevant knowledge and experience, it is very difficult, if not impossible, to evaluate messages from reading.

Reasoning Skills. Background knowledge and experience are necessary but not sufficient prerequisites for critical reading. To be a critical reader also requires logical thinking.

Attitude. A questioning attitude is essential to critical reading and thinking. Critical readers constantly test what they read against previous understanding and logical criteria.

The process of critical reading requires three steps: comprehension, analysis, and evaluation. Readers must employ each of these (or consciously omit) before accepting as worthwhile the message of any written material.

Comprehension. Critical readers must understand what writers are saying before responding to their information or interpretations.

Reading furnishes our mind only with materials of knowledge; it is thinking that makes what we read ours.
—John Locke

Analysis. Readers seek evidence to support their evaluation of the writer's ideas and style. Expository material requires readers to determine whether the writer's purpose is informational or persuasive. Analytical questions for reading expository material critically include the following.
- Is the writer an expert on the subject?
- What is the writer's purpose? Does the writer have a hidden motive, some purposes beyond what is stated? How might the writer benefit if the reader accepts this message?
- What assumptions does the writer make? Are they valid?
- What facts are presented? Are they accurate as far as can be determined? Are they relevant to the message?
- Do the facts support the conclusions presented?

In reading literature, critical readers analyze thematic and character development, use of imagery and symbols, plot development, writer style, and the relationships between form and content. See *A Guide to Curriculum Planning in Language Arts* for a more extensive discussion of literary elements and approaches.

Evaluation. Evaluation involves comparing the results of one's analysis to pre-established standards and deciding how well they have been satisfied. Readers may conclude that an author has made a strong or weak or perhaps a mixed case for a given message. A literary work may be a significant work of art, likely to endure and affect many other readers, or it may seem merely a passing diversion. Good critical readers are able to formulate and substantiate such judgement.

How Can Critical Reading and Thinking Be Developed?

The research literature suggests several broad guidelines for effective teaching of critical reading and thinking.
- An attitude of critical thinking needs to be fostered at all stages and in all areas of the curriculum.
- Instruction in critical reading and thinking requires an ongoing commitment of both teachers and students. Brief units or exercises will not produce significant, long-lasting results.
- Instruction in critical analysis and evaluation should focus on content that students have already been studying. Emphasis should be placed on using the information rather than merely acquiring it.
- Opportunities should be provided to adapt acquired critical reading techniques to new situations.
- Numerous and continuing opportunities should be provided for practice in critical reading.

Although most young children lack the reasoning ability and depth of knowledge of more advanced learners, there is evidence to suggest they are nonetheless able to carry out rudimentary forms of critical thinking. Stauffer's Directed Reading Thinking Activity (DRTA) (see page 96) can be helpful in developing critical readers. In a DRTA students are encouraged to use their knowledge and experiences as well as such

... helping students to comprehend meanings through relating them to what they already know, to talk or write about these meanings, to use them to make decisions, and to judge them.
–Margaret Early (1985)

reading aids as titles and pictures to make predictions about the outcomes of a story. As reading proceeds, students are encouraged to check their predictions against new information in the story and, if necessary, revise their predictions. In this way, emphasis is placed on learning to analyze relevant information and to check the logic of one's guesses. Reading is approached as a problem-solving activity that can be interesting and creative rather than as a search for the one right answer to a literal-level question.

For more mature reading students (usually middle grades and advanced), comparative reading assignments offer an excellent means of promoting critical responses to printed text. By comparing and contrasting different perspectives on a single topic, students become aware that an issue can be treated in different ways. They also sharpen their analytical skills as they identify and categorize likenesses and differences to gather evidence for judging the strengths and weaknesses of different texts. In such assignments students might be asked to compare a subject's treatment in different textbooks—popular magazines, trade-books, books, or reference books. They might compare different styles of writing—biography and fictional, or straight news accounts, editorials, critiques, or by-lined reports in mass media publications. At all reading stages teachers can foster critical reading and thinking by modeling behaviors of critical thinkers and readers as they interact with students in group or individual learning situations.

How Can Critical Reading and Thinking Skills Be Assessed?

Informal assessment of critical reading and thinking can be made by noting the quality of class discussion, evaluating oral or written responses to critical reading assignments, and judging answers to critical reading and thinking problems in all content areas.

Summary

The ultimate goal of critical thinking and reading instruction is to produce independent, self-directed critical reading and thinking behaviors. To do so, students need to be taught to think and read critically, to identify and defend their own criteria for evaluation, and to judge their own effectiveness as critical thinkers and readers.

Critical Reading and Thinking

Stage	Teacher	Student
Emergent Reading	Encourages how and why questions	Asks how and why questions about stories and events
Beginning Reading	Helps children establish simple criteria to evaluate a character's actions and feelings	Uses background experience to judge the behavior of story characters
	Helps children develop criteria for identifying a good story	Compares stories and expresses a preference
	Helps children see that personal likes and dislikes can influence thinking	Begins to recognize that personal likes and dislikes may create errors in judgement
	Helps children understand that a single experience with another person or situation is usually inadequate for reaching a conclusion about that individual or situation	Recognizes when story characters reach incorrect conclusions based on limited evidence
	Helps children develop criteria for determining whether a story is true or based on fantasy	Detects evidence indicating whether a story is true or make believe
	Guides students to use the Directed Reading Thinking Activity	Uses the Directed Reading Thinking Activity with guidance
Reading for Consolidation	Introduces students to criteria for testing whether a statement is fact or opinion	Identifies clues which indicate whether a statement is fact or opinion
	Introduces students to such attributes of good informational writing as accuracy and completeness. Engages students in comparative reading activities to provide practice in using these criteria	Compares, contrasts, and judges the relative worth of information sources on the same topic
	Guides students to use Directed Reading Thinking Activity independently	Develops ability to use Directed Reading Thinking Activity independently
	Introduces students to common propaganda techniques	Recognizes and explains how words and phrases are used in a selection to persuade the reader to embrace a particular point of view

Critical Reading and Thinking *(continued)*

Stage	Teacher	Student
Reading to Learn the New	Engages students in identification and analysis of literary devices and the impression they create Introduces students to text selection techniques – searching for indications of a writer's background and credentials – studying the preface for information on the writer's goals – checking the publication date and citations for clues to relevancy and reliablity	Analyzes and judges with guidance the effects of various literary techniques Evaluates source credibility and reliability with given criteria and shares findings with peers and teachers
Reading for Independence	Demonstrates and provides practice in logically analyzing text material and other reading Teaches students to view conclusions from more than one point of view Gives students experiences in relating background knowledge and critical thinking abilities in order to question and refute claims in advertising and one-sided presentations of controversial issues Encourages and rewards students for raising critical questions and for developing and defending their own criteria for making judgements	Evaluates source credibility and reliability. Begins to apply tests of logic and scientific reasoning to informational and persuasive writing Analyzes materials from different perspectives Resists emotional appeal of propaganda. Uses background knowledge and questioning to evaluate advertising and one-sided presentations of controversial issues Begins to probe materials using own criteria Reflects on reading
Mature Reading	Engages students in application of various critical reading behaviors through modeling, in class discussions, and written assignments	Internalizes and automatically applies the probing questions – the reliability of a purported authority – an author's assumptions (explicit and implicit) – whether a hypothesis or theory is warranted – whether statements are vague or specific – whether conclusions follow from the evidence presented

Why Should Writing Be Included in Reading Instruction?

Students who regularly write as part of the reading instruction program come to realize that they as well as the authors have something to communicate. Both reading and writing depend upon comprehension, and thus require students to think, analyze, synthesize, and organize. Both require students to use background knowledge, including knowledge of the language and how it functions. Writing helps them continue to develop a sense of reading as a process of comprehension.

What Kinds of Writing Are Appropriate?

Various kinds of writing are helpful to students in developing their comprehension skills. Expository writing communicates information, instructions, explanations, or some combination. Some writing is an attempt to advise or persuade others. Another kind of writing allows students opportunities for self expression; it includes writing in journals and diaries where the focus of interest is likely to be on the writer. Imaginative writing emphasizes literary purposes.

Students should be exposed to good models of writing. When given opportunities to write, they should be encouraged to use earlier listening and reading experiences to develop their own styles. Emphasis should be placed on writing as a means of learning—a form of experience itself—rather than just a means of displaying acquired knowledge. Thus students should perceive writing as much more than a mechanical task such as providing short answers or filling in blanks. Writing is an excellent way to develop and assess comprehension as well as a way for students to organize and express their ideas, emotions, and experiences. Teachers need to create situations in which writing serves the healthy, ongoing desire of students to communicate what they know and feel. The stages of writing—prewriting, writing, revising, and editing—should be included in the reading instruction process. These processes are presented in detail in *A Guide for Curriculum Planning in the Language Arts.*

How Should Writing Be Included in Reading Instruction

Like reading, writing is a developmental process that does not follow specific pattern characteristics at a particular age or grade level. Instead, certain general achievement patterns suggest a progression that most students follow in their writing development. Students at any one reading stage will vary greatly in writing ability.

The stages of writing occur along more or less parallel lines to those of reading. At the Emergent Reading stage, children can be observed scribbling as they pretend to read. As they gain a better understanding of concepts of print and meaning, young children often begin to conceive and use invented spellings. It is a good idea to allow them to experiment with print and to provide opportunities for pre-readers to dictate stories. Dictation in the early reading stages is ideally suited for children who have many ideas and experiences to communicate yet are not adept with the mechanics of writing.

At the Beginning Reading stage, students need suggestions to stimulate their writing, which will be based both on personal and literary experiences. Using children's literature in the reading program is an excellent way to integrate reading and writing. It provides familiar stories for students to draw upon in creative writing exercises.

Two distinct trends emerge from these beginning stages of writing. Students begin to write more complex sentences, and their writing includes more specific detail. The subsequent stages are characterized by increased sentence length, a greater variety of pronouns and synonyms, more precise words, and increased overall length of compositions. The content of students' writing also changes. There is a change from static description to narration of events, movement from focus on self to concern for others, a development from single to multiple events, an increasing use of dialogue, increasing use of details, and the addition of minor events and of explanation.

Teachers need to devise exercises and activities that allow students to express ideas based on personal experiences. They also need to provide opportunities for students to write for audiences other than the teacher and for purposes other than evaluation. It is important to supplement traditional workbook exercises with creative writing activities at all grade levels. The following purposes can be achieved by integrating writing with reading instruction.

- Developing or reinforcing comprehension by having students write predictions, main ideas, and critical analyses and evaluations
- Providing practice in specific reading and studying skills and strategies by having students write pre-reading and post-reading comprehension questions, summaries, and study notes
- Increasing sensitivity to writing conventions (mechanics), styles, and organizational patterns by having students dictate language experience stories
    - using story grammar framework in writing narrative;
    - changing the point of view, conclusion, or organizational structure of a text.

How Can Writing Be Used in Assessment?

Writing can play an important role in assessing and diagnosing how well students comprehend texts they read. Writing provides valuable clues in assessing the effectiveness of the reading program.

Research with very young children on invented spelling suggests that children's early experiences with writing may promote the development of letter-sound knowledge.
–C. Chomsky

A program which integrates reading and writing is successful if students can do the following.

- Demonstrate reading comprehension by writing
  - a story map
  - a summary of a passage
  - main idea and supporting details
- Predict (in writing) further events or the conclusion of a story
- Demonstrate understanding of organization and phonic skills in their writing
- Write responses to questions about reading

Summary

Learning to read can be enhanced by writing just as learning to write can be enhanced by reading. In the same way that strategic readers become self-actuating and independent in comprehending, they develop a personal style and strategies for responding in writing. A strong reading program will include writing as an essential component. Teachers need to foster and reinforce the reading-writing connection.

Responding in Writing

Stage	Teacher	Student
Emergent Reading	Uses language experience approach, including children's key words, individual stories, and group experience charts	Sees relationship of oral language to reading and writing Discovers that ideas can be expressed in print and read and reread Begins to understand the concepts of letter, word, sentence, and other conventions of writing, including punctuation and capitalization Develops motivation for learning to read through reading-dictated experience stories
	Uses predictable books as a model for children's writing	Dictates predictable stories
	Provides time for students to share their key words and dictated stories	Develops self-confidence in the ability to read and practices oral reading skills
	Uses children's own words and stories to introduce beginning reading skills (rhyming, letter recognition, beginning consonant sounds)	Recognizes letters of the alphabet and becomes aware of sound/symbol relationships
	Maintains a writing center in the classroom	Experiments with writing independently (scribbling, writing name, practicing the letters of the alphabet)
Beginning Reading	Supplements the basal reading program with language experience activities	Dictates stories and rereads dictated stories
	Encourages children to write on their own	Describes pictures with phrases or sentences Composes simple experience stories using invented spelling Increases writing vocabulary
	Provides opportunities for book projects (drawing, sharing, discussing)	Develops increasing desire to share stories as writing ability increases Responds in various ways to books read
	Expands classroom writer center so that children's writing can be displayed and read	Becomes aware that reading and writing are purposeful activities

Stage	Teacher	Student
Beginning Reading *(continued)*	Uses children's literature as a model for students' writing	Begins to develop a schema for story structure which serves as an aid in writing narrative material
	Uses informational books as a model for students' writing	Writes informational stories
Reading for Consolidation	Integrates writing with reading activities (teaching students how to summarize or paraphrase a reading passage)	Demonstrates comprehension by writing summaries or paraphrasing passages Uses critical thinking skills to organize thoughts in writing
	Encourages children to respond to reading materials through writing (book reviews, letters to editors, or authors)	Shares thoughts and feelings about material read in writing
	Provides opportunities for students to write using various forms (drama, poetry, letter writing)	Uses various forms of writing to communicate and respond appropriately to a variety of audiences
	Teaches students to conduct simple research projects related to content area of personal interest	Organizes information for written research project
	Assigns written report as a culminating research product	Uses basic paragraph structure, main idea, and supporting detail to write a short report
Reading to Learn the New	Provides time for students to write daily	Keeps journal for recording thoughts, ideas, and concerns
	Encourages students to respond in writing to what they have read (summarizing, paraphrasing, and elaborating)	Shares writing with peers and others outside the classroom
	Relates writing assignments to students' interests	Chooses topics for writing and does research to gather information about topic
	Instructs students on ways of gathering and organizing information for a written report	Shares information with peers, organizes information, and prepares written report

Responding in Writing *(continued)*

Stage	Teacher	Student
Reading to Learn the New *(continued)*	Teaches students to use the dictionary and thesaurus for elaboration of word meanings	Edits, revises, and prepares final report for publication
Reading for Independence	Provides time for writing	Adds comments, thoughts, ideas, and concerns to journal
	Encourages students to explore varying viewpoints on a subject	Analyzes materials with varying viewpoints in writing
	Guides students to make judgments about materials read	Makes judgments regarding viewpoints in writing and synthesizes in terms of own criteria in writing
	Directs the student to reading and writing activities which require thinking, analyzing, evaluating, and organizing subject matter	Responds in writing
Mature Reading	Guides or reinforces reading and writing activities which require thinking, analyzing, evaluating, and organizing subject matter	Demonstrates competency in reading and writing to create new knowledge Develops a personal style of writing

Why Is Developing Attitudes and Interests Important?

Students' attitudes and interests should be taken into consideration when planning for reading instruction. A balanced reading program should encourage students to value reading as a pleasurable and enriching experience. Instilling in students a desire to read is just as important as teaching them how to read and will aid the learning process. If students are to develop life-long reading habits, they must experience the excitement and personal fulfillment that reading brings as well as its practical benefits.

Reading can enrich people's understanding of themselves and of the world.
–Reading Report Card (1985)

What Types of Activities Should Be Included?

A variety of reading materials must be provided so students can experience the different ways reading can be personally rewarding. Reading to relax, to satisfy curiosity, and to gain new information are important benefits. Teachers can provide many opportunities for students to select materials to read that match their personal interests and activities. A comprehensive reading program will include planned time during the school day for recreational and independent reading.

How Can Attitudes and Interests Be Developed?

Even though there is a wide variety of individual differences, there are some activities common to all stages that need to be emphasized. Teachers at every grade level and in every subject area should do the following.
● Read aloud to students
● Model desirable reading behavior
● Provide time for personal reading
● Make available and encourage students to read a wide range of materials
● Encourage personal reading
Additional suggestions for developing interests and positive attitudes are listed in the scope and sequence.

How Can Reading Attitudes and Interests Be Assessed?

Teachers can talk with students and observe what nonassigned books or magazines they are reading. They can discuss books with students in individual conferences to learn about their interests and feelings concerning reading as well as to communicate their concerns for the students as individuals. Informal observations and personal interactions may be the best means for gathering information about students' attitudes and interests toward reading and can be useful in evaluating the impact of personal reading in the curriculum. The following questions will help curriculum planners and teachers evaluate the effects of a personal reading program.

- What is the usage of library books by various classes or individuals?
- How much independent reading is done at home, as reported by parents?
- Does information from a public librarian indicate enthusiasm toward reading among students? In what special areas?
- What comments are heard from students about books they are reading independently?
- What is the quality of choices made by students during silent, independent reading times?
- How much use is made of independent reading in various subject areas?

Section 9 describes how one district developed and evaluated a school-wide reading time. Some suggested ways for assessing interests and attitudes are listed below.

- Interest inventories
- Attitude questionnaires
- Interviews both structured and informal
- Observation checklists
- School and public library circulation records
- Students' personal reading records
- Autobiographies
- Skits and other creative presentations based on reading
- Bulletin board displays
- Discussion of current events, sports, and films made from books

Summary

As students grow toward becoming independent readers, it is important for teachers to model and encourage reading as a life-long activity of choice. By providing opportunities and rewarding such reading, teachers help students develop positive attitudes toward reading as a means of life-long enjoyment. A love of books and the enthusiasm for reading are established at a very early age; positive attitudes should be systematically nurtured by teachers and parents throughout the stages of reading development. This nurturing includes reading aloud to students, modeling desirable reading behaviors, providing time for personal choice reading, and stimulating interests.

The secret of it all lies in the parents' reading aloud to and with the child.
–Huey, 1908

Attitudes and Interests

Stage	Teacher	Student
Emergent Reading	Reads aloud to students Talks with children about what has been read Utilizes language experience approach Reads dictated words and sentences Writes dictated words and sentences Develops interest centers (book center, listening center, writing center)	Shows pleasure in being read to Pretends to read, talks about story and pictures Is aware that spoken words have value and, when written, can be read by others Develops a desire to read for pleasure Develops self-confidence in ability to read Chooses to use the reading, writing, and listening centers during independent activity time
Beginning Reading	Reads regularly to students from a variety of materials (poetry, narrative, informational) Provides a reading corner with an interesting book display Allows students to self-select according to interests Provides regular opportunities for silent reading Models reading during silent reading time Provides time for students to extend and share reading and writing experiences Schedules regular trips to school and and community libraries Encourages children to get library cards and to enroll in summer reading programs	Demonstrates an active interest in reading Uses free time to browse and read independently Chooses books of personal interests Participates in SSR (sustained silent reading) Shares personal responses to books with other children in a variety of ways Selects materials that are both confirming and satisfying Reads and rereads tradebooks (fiction and non-fiction)

Attitudes and Interests

Stage	Teacher	Student
Reading for Consolidation	Reads aloud to students	Shows enjoyment in being read to
	Provides time for silent reading Models silent reading	Participates in SSR
	Provides reading materials to match children's interests	Reads materials to match personal interests
	Provides trade books to enrich content-area study	Reads trade books on topics related to materials in content areas
	Guides students' use of library	Seeks help from teacher and librarian in learning library skills
	Instructs students on how to read reference and content-area materials	Uses children's dictionaries and encyclopedias
	Provides bulletin boards, books, and writing and listening centers to encourage reading and writing	Participates in reading and writing center activities
Reading to Learn the New	Reads aloud to students	Shows interest in being read to
	Provides time for silent reading Models silent reading	Participates in SSR
	Surveys student-reading interests and habits	Reads materials to match interests
		Shares materials of interest with other students
	Provides materials and reading activities to match interests	
	Introduces students to a wide variety of fiction and nonfiction materials	Begins to select books about a variety of topics
	Provides trade books to enrich content-area study	Reads trade books on topics related to materials in content areas
	Makes accessible a wide range of content-related fiction and nonfiction materials of varying difficulty	
Reading for Independence	Makes vigorous effort to spark enthusiasm and further develop reading tastes by – reading aloud to students – modeling reading behaviors – providing time for reading	Participates in SSR time provided by school Shares common interests with peers and teachers Reads a variety of materials for different viewpoints

Stage	Teacher	Student
Reading for Independence *(continued)*	Exposes students to a variety of popular, high quality tradebooks, magazines, and newspapers for both current and future use Encourages use of library and reference materials for gathering information	Selects materials of high quality interest for personal reading Uses library as a valuable resource for gathering information for all content areas
Mature Reading	Provides opportunities to increase the breadth and depth of students' reading, including such options as – independent study – book clubs – study groups – special reading classes – arrangements with local businesses, colleges, universities, and library loan networks	Exhibits a maturity of interests, depth of understanding, and wide range of reading choices Uses a wide variety of resources Demonstrates and models reading to others

Implementation

Analyzing the Curriculum 5

Introduction

After describing a curriculum and providing suggestions for instruction, school districts must address implementation of the curriculum. Transforming written concepts into classroom instruction is a challenging task. *A Guide to Curriculum Planning* outlines steps for incorporating any curriculum into a particular school or district. This section highlights important steps and considerations unique to implementing a reading program.

Assessing Current Programs

In a well designed reading program, mastering the parts does not become an end in itself, but a means to an end, and there is a proper balance between practice of the parts and practice of the whole.
–Becoming a Nation of Readers

Curriculum implementation should be based upon an assessment of needs. Educators need to determine carefully what goals of reading are currently being addressed, what goals are effective, and what changes are needed. This process involves considering which current practices fit within the newly proposed framework, which do not, and which need modification. To guide a curriculum committee in this process, a detailed list is included in table 4. This checklist, which addresses basic considerations relevant to a research-based reading program, is based on the entire contents of this guide and is best used in conjunction with the guide. It is highly recommended that in using the checklist the reading committee involve classroom teachers, administrators, subject area specialists, and community representatives at both elementary and secondary levels. For any program, a sense of ownership as well as a sense of responsibility for maintaining it helps to strengthen staff and community commitment and to eliminate a sense of threat among those facing change. All involved should be encouraged to view the checklist as a tool for examining the strengths and weaknesses of the existing program. Using this list annually will allow opportunities for reading specialists and others concerned with curriculum development to assess progress in meeting short-term and long-term goals for the reading program.

Table 4 ■

Checklist for Assessing Reading Program

Rate each item according to the following scale:

0	Not Present
1	Somewhat Effective
2	Very Effective

Reader, Text, Context

The Strategic Reader. How effective is your reading program in developing mature, independent readers?

1. Students are given opportunities to progress through the stages of reading development at their own pace. 0 1 2

2. Students are given reading opportunities to automatize various skills. 0 1 2

3. Students are given opportunities and instruction to develop strategies to self-monitor comprehension. 0 1 2
   a. Set purpose 0 1 2
   b. Evaluate reading task 0 1 2
   c. Use text structure to organize reading 0 1 2
   d. Use background knowledge 0 1 2
   e. Adapt rate 0 1 2
   f. Reflect on reading 0 1 2

4. Students are self-motivated to do outside, free reading. 0 1 2

5. Students are aware of their abilities and deficiencies. 0 1 2

The Text. How effective are the materials used in reading instruction?

6. The reading program uses a variety of materials.
   a. Basal readers 0 1 2
   b. Narrative materials 0 1 2
   c. Expository materials 0 1 2
   d. Trade books 0 1 2
   e. Other reading materials ("real life" texts) 0 1 2

7. Textbooks are selected through consideration of important qualities in aiding reading development.
   a. Structure 0 1 2
   b. Coherence 0 1 2
   c. Unity 0 1 2
   d. Appropriateness 0 1 2

8. The reading scope and sequence goes beyond that presented by the basal teacher's manual. 0 1 2

9. A library (IMC) is an integral part of a total reading program. 0 1 2

Table 4 *(continued)*

Checklist for Assessing Reading Program

0	Not Present
1	Somewhat Effective
2	Very Effective

10. A library offers a wide variety of print and nonprint materials to encourage reading.   0   1   2

The Context. Is the present school reading environment conducive to developing strategic readers?

11. Reading situations encourage self-selection of reading by students.   0   1   2

12. Reading situations span the entire curriculum across all subject areas.   0   1   2

13. Reading situations integrate language arts instruction (reading, writing, discussing, clarifying, organizing) with subject-area material.   0   1   2

14. Reading tasks require both general and specific reading strategies.   0   1   2

15. Reading tasks necessitate transfer of strategies from familiar to new reading materials.   0   1   2

16. The school environment provides ample opportunity for silent reading, such as
    a. regularly scheduled times   0   1   2
    b. conducive atmosphere (quiet, comfortable)   0   1   2
    c. silent reading encouraged through modeling   0   1   2

17. Students are assured opportunities to interact in reflection, discussion, and evaluation of their reading.   0   1   2

Instruction

Instructional Approaches. What instructional approaches are currently being used by the staff?

1. Instruction exemplifies that the best practice for learning to read is to read.   0   1   2

2. Instruction provides a greater percentage of time for reading itself, rather than for teaching skills.   0   1   2

3. Instruction focuses upon learners instead of upon the program itself.   0   1   2

4. Instruction assesses students' abilities and needs as they relate to stages of reading development.   0   1   2

5. Instruction focuses on what students need to know rather than what they have previously learned.   0   1   2

6. Instruction provides application of skills for automaticity.   0   1   2

7. Instruction guides students to identify words using grapho-phonic, snytax, or semantic clues.   0 1 2

8. Instruction emphasizes comprehension.   0 1 2

9. Instruction assesses background knowledge of students.   0 1 2

10. Instruction incorporates guidance in developing self-monitoring behavior.   0 1 2

11. Instruction develops critical thinking skills.   0 1 2

12. Instruction promotes application of reading strategies in "real life" contexts.   0 1 2

13. Instruction moves students from dependence to independence.   0 1 2

14. Instruction provides for the diverse needs, interests, and abilities of all students.   0 1 2

15. Instruction includes
    a. word meaning and analysis   0 1 2
    b. text organization (expository and narrative)   0 1 2
    c. critical reading and thinking   0 1 2
    d. responding in writing   0 1 2
    e. developing interests and attitudes   0 1 2
    f. developing strategic behavior   0 1 2

Evaluation. What is the range and effectiveness of evaluation methods currently included in the reading program?

16. Evaluation methods provide continuous feedback for determining program effectiveness and needs.   0 1 2

17. Evaluation methods include gathering of both formal and informal data.   0 1 2

18. Evaluation methods include both affective and cognitive measures.   0 1 2

19. Evaluation methods emphasize teacher judgment.   0 1 2

20. Evaluation methods include student reactions.   0 1 2

21. Evaluation methods include parent and community input (surveys, conferences).   0 1 2

22. Evaluation results are analyzed and used for instructional improvement.   0 1 2

Checklist for Assessing Reading Program

0	Not Present
1	Somewhat Effective
2	Very Effective

Staff

Teachers. How effective are teachers in instructing and encouraging reading development?

1. Teachers demonstrate professional decision-making abilities.
a. Assess stages of student reading development	0	1	2
b. Analyze text and task	0	1	2
c. Identify skills and strategies students require to accomplish task	0	1	2
d. Plan appropriate and varied instructional activities	0	1	2

2. Teachers use a variety of instructional techniques and methodologies.   0   1   2

3. Teachers model appropriate reading behaviors.
a. Demonstrate effective use of reading strategies	0	1	2
b. Read aloud to students	0	1	2
c. Encourage students to interact in relation to reading	0	1	2
d. Model the enjoyment of silent reading	0	1	2

4. Teachers organize flexible groups for varied instructional purposes.   0   1   2

5. Teachers plan reading lessons using supplemental enrichment materials.   0   1   2

6. Teachers provide appropriate independent reading activities.   0   1   2

7. Teachers provide silent reading time.   0   1   2

8. Teachers provide conference opportunities for students and parents.   0   1   2

Reading Specialists. What services are currently being provided by a reading specialists?

9. The reading specialist is used, for the most part, as a resource person.   0   1   2

10. The reading specialist provides overall leadership in development and articulation of K-12 reading program.   0   1   2

11. The reading specialist keeps abreast of new research, methodology, and materials.   0   1   2

12. The reading specialist communicates new research concepts and materials to teachers, administrators, and school board members.   0   1   2

13. The reading specialist demonstrates effective teaching strategies.   0   1   2

14. The reading specialist assists subject-area teachers to incorporate reading instruction into content areas.   0   1   2

15. The reading specialist demonstrates appropriate diagnostic and evaluation techniques.   0   1   2

16. The reading specialist provides inservice opportunities.   0   1   2

17. The reading specialist assists in development of programs for students with special needs.   0   1   2

18. The reading specialist guides parents in ways to promote reading development at home.   0   1   2

19. The reading specialist involves and trains instructional aides and volunteers who work in the reading program.   0   1   2

Staff Development. How effective is the present staff development program in reading?

20. Staff development is an essential component of the reading program.   0   1   2

21. Staff development involves acquainting teachers with new research methodology and materials.   0   1   2

22. Inservice sessions demonstrate practical application of research and theory.   0   1   2

23. Inservice is an ongoing process entailing preparation, presentation, and follow-up.   0   1   2

24. Staff development includes preparation for textbook selection.

25. Staff development provides opportunity for curriculum development and implementation.   0   1   2

Administrative Support. How supportive is the administration of the reading program?

26. The administration and school board members recognize and support reading instruction as a priority.   0   1   2

27. Adequate funds are budgeted to plan, initiate, and maintain a quality reading program.   0   1   2

28. The administration supports a balanced reading program.   0   1   2

29. The administration encourages teacher involvement and decision making.   0   1   2

30. The administration supports teachers in their efforts to improve reading instruction.   0   1   2

Planning for Staff Development

Changes in the approach to reading comprehension instruction, suggested by recent research and by this guide, require thorough and ongoing staff development. Although new materials and techniques are still being developed and refined, the task of translating the new model for comprehension into classroom planning and teaching is a necessary part of the curriculum design. Inservice is one means of translating research into practice. As better texts and other teaching aids appear and accounts of more useful techniques are published, school districts with sound programs of staff development will be able to incorporate them efficiently into their programs.

Effective Inservice

The most effective inservice programs are built upon research and provide teachers with practical suggestions and models for applying that research to their daily teaching.

Studies of staff development programs have indicated that inservice sessions are most effective for teachers when certain considerations are followed. A published list of suggestions based on these studies is found in Appendix H. The following are characteristics of quality inservice programs in reading instruction.

*Schools should provide for the continuing professional development of teachers.
–Becoming a Nation of Readers*

• Inservice is helpful when preceded by a careful assessment of current practices and teaching needs. The checklist in table 4 details items to consider when making such assessment before inservice sessions are scheduled and planned. Classroom teachers should be involved in the assessment so that their needs are addressed.

• The single most important factor affecting the success of staff development programs is having the support of the district administrator and school principals. This support includes adequate funding for inservice sessions as well as time, space, and encouragement. If teachers perceive a commitment by administrators to quality inservice sessions, they will approach the sessions in a purposeful and optimistic manner.

• Inservice should consist of more than single sessions. Two or more sessions separated by at least one week appear to have a more positive effect on teaching than an intensive, one-shot approach that does not allow opportunity for teachers to try new practices, modify them to suit individual situations, and gradually adapt them to existing instructional programs.

• Detailed presentation of concepts and facts, including demonstrations (modeling) where relevant, is more useful than abstract, generalized lectures. Group discussion and teacher involvement in concrete activities seem to be of particular value when new material is being presented. Opportunties to practice a new skill and receive feedback through such activities as role playing, peer observation, and classroom coaching are advised.

• Inservice sessions should occur in an atmosphere of trust and collaboration. Since active participation is desired, teachers will need to feel a supportive environment in which questions are encouraged and guidance provided in learning and applying new strategies.

• Inservice sessions should be evaluated and an effort made to follow up on the results. Evaluations may be accomplished by getting written comments from the participants immediately after the inservice. It is important that participants and administrators be informed of the results.

Summary

To have the best chance of affecting teaching and thus serve developing readers, a staff development program should

• focus on concrete, specific strategies rather than only emphasizing theory;

• emphasize demonstrations, with opportunities for participants to practice new skills and receive feedback;

• be individualized, responding to the particular needs of each participant or small groups of teachers;

• be ongoing and thoughtfully spaced, as opposed to single-session "injections";

• involve school principals as participants;

• include teachers in planning, evaluating, and making necessary modifications.

Planning for Instruction 6

Research on Reading Comprehension Instruction

The knowledge is now available to make worthwhile improvements in reading throughout the United States. If the practices seen in the classrooms of the best teachers in the best schools could be introduced everywhere, improvements in reading would be dramatic.

The recent report, *Becoming a Nation of Readers* (Anderson), suggests that although many of this nation's students are not skilled readers, they could be if more teachers change the way they teach reading. The report suggests there is now enough knowledge about reading instruction to make worthwhile improvements in reading. The following pages report on research and outline practices which will help local reading committees and classroom teachers implement research-based comprehension instruction. Many of these practices are not yet a part of the teacher's manuals.

In her first study, in 1979, Dolores Durkin focused on the kind and amount of reading comprehension instruction that existed in grades 3-6 during reading and social studies classes. Her results included the following.

• Out of the 11,587 minutes of reading classes observed, only 45 minutes went to comprehension instruction. The average length of comprehension instruction within a class period was only 3.7 minutes.

• No comprehension instruction was taught in social studies classes.

• The amount of time spent testing comprehension was ten times greater than the amount of time spent instructing comprehension.

• Large amounts of time went to giving and checking written assignments. "Teachers keep their classes so perpetually occupied with busy work that neither chaos nor learning takes place."

• In summary, ". . . teachers were mentioners, assignment givers, assignment checkers, and interrogators." They quickly gave a number of assignments and asked lots of questions.

These observations led Durkin to her second study, in 1981, in which she read, word for word, the basal manuals from kindergarten through grade 6 to identify what the manuals offered for comprehension instruction. She also wanted to see whether a connection existed between what she had observed in the classrooms and what was contained in manuals. The results of her analysis were as follows.

• The most instances of instruction found in one entire series were 128. The least was 60. She was generous in her definition of instruction and included single sentence statements such as "Lead the children to generalize that . . . . Help the students to understand that . . . ." Many instances of instruction were simply definitions such as "the main idea is the most important idea in the paragraph."

• Suggestions for review were typically one sentence long. The frequency of review appeared to have *NO* connection with the difficulty or importance of the skill. Review was spaced throughout the manual in a random manner.

• Practice was in the form of worksheets and ditto-sheet exercises. The tendency was to focus on brief pieces of text even when what was to be practiced seemed to call for larger units of text. Typically, one practice was followed by another for something entirely different.

● Application was seldom related to reading connected text. Just as with practice, application tended to be with brief pieces of text even when the skill to be applied called for larger units of text.

In her third study, in 1984, Durkin observed teachers in grades 1, 3, and 5, to answer the question, "Is there a match between what elementary teachers do and what basal reader manuals recommend?" She found the following patterns.

● Little or no time went to teaching new vocabulary, background information, or prereading questions.

● Classroom management and control were considered as important as what helped the students become better readers.

● There was an abundance of group oral reading which was used as much as a device for controlling students as for teaching them.

● Considerable time went to comprehension assessment questions and written practice assignments.

● The most generous use of time was for written practice. Every assignment referred to in the skill development segments of the teacher's manuals was used and others were added.

● Most of the comprehension questions in the manual were asked. The greatest concern was for right answers. When a student answered the question correctly, the teacher proceeded to the next question. When the student answered it incorrectly, the teacher called on other students until a right answer was obtained. Then another question was asked.

● None of the teachers appeared to teach diagnostically; that is, identify instructional needs and teach to those needs. Instead they gave the next assignments in the book.

● There were a number of times the teachers did not adhere to the manual. The usual reasons given were either not enough time or lack of importance of what was being suggested.

The picture this research gives of reading instruction is that there is almost no comprehension instruction in classrooms; that the basal reader teacher's manuals exert a strong influence on teaching; and that many teachers use the manuals unselectively while others use them selectively but with no overall instructional plan.

Teachers as Decision Makers

Classroom teachers at all levels make many decisions each school day that affect the quality of their teaching and students' learning. These decisions include organization of the classroom, allocation of time and resources, development of lessons, development of curriculum, and presentation of lessons. During presentation of lessons, teachers are constantly assessing the situation, processing information about the situation, making decisions about what to do next, guiding action on the basis of these decisions, and observing the effects of the action on the students. The discussion and guidelines that follow are presented here to give direction to teachers in making decisions when developing and presenting comprehension lessons.

Teaching Cycle

The foundation for making instructional decisions is the Wisconsin Model for Reading Comprehension, the developmental stages, and the framework for developing strategic behavior. Guidelines for making instructional decisions developed from this information are presented graphically in the Teaching Cycle (figure 5) to illustrate how these guidelines influence planning, teaching, guiding, and expecting independence in reading lessons. The teaching cycle consists of five basic components.

- Planning for teaching
- Teaching
- Independent practice/application - narrow contexts
- Independent practice/application - wide contexts
- Assessment

Figure 5

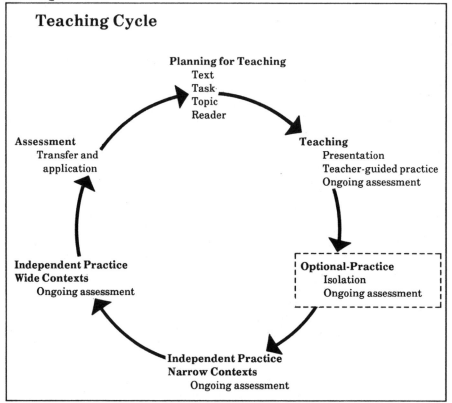

84

The teaching cycle can strengthen reading instruction by focusing teachers' attention on students' needs at each step of the cycle rather than only on lesson plan outlines in manuals. It helps teachers plan balanced lessons. The framework of the cycle is a constant reminder to focus attention on *application* of strategies and skills through the development of strategic behavior.

Planning for Teaching. During the planning for teaching stage, teachers consider the knowledge about text, topic, and task which students bring to the situation; the strategies and skills that need to be developed; and the students' interests and attitudes. Teachers consider these factors in relationship to the lesson context, classroom context, and curriculum context.

Curriculum development is not a complete process until the curriculum is used in the classroom.

Based on this information, teachers select objectives for the lesson. Usually there will be at least two objectives for a comprehension lesson, one for word meaning and one for the comprehension strategy(ies). Teachers may include other objectives as appropriate to the students and situation. This step is probably the most time consuming and crucial to the success of the lesson.

Teaching of the Skill. Next comes the teaching of the skill or strategy which includes the presentation and teacher-guided practice. During the presentation, the teacher presents the information to be learned, probably using modeling, explanation, and discovery, or a combination. It is during this step that students find out what they are going to learn, how to do it, why, and when it is useful. This is followed by teacher-guided practice with appropriate examples for practicing the skill strategy. The teacher's role should shift gradually from information giving to coaching so that the students are taking on more and more responsibility. When the teacher judges that the students are practicing more correct than incorrect responses (around 65 percent - 75 percent accuracy) or understanding the strategy and skill well enough to work on their own, they are ready to move to independent practice.

Independent Practice. Independent practice should include practice of the strategy and skill in both narrow and wide contexts. Narrow context is chosen for the specific lesson, which is typically the basal reader selection and other short practice materials. Wide contexts represent realistic settings for using the strategy and skill so that students can transfer and apply their knowledge to a variety of reading situations. Students need to be encouraged to integrate all of their strategies and skills into wide contexts through analyzing, planning, monitoring, and regulating their comprehension.

Optional Practice. An optional type of isolated practice may be necessary for some students who need additional concrete examples, who may not have learned a prerequisite skill, or who need to gain more confidence for using a skill or strategy. This kind of isolated practice should be followed immediately by practice in whole texts, both narrow and wide contexts.

I would like to propose a new model for the 1980s—a model in which the teacher assumes a more central and active role in providing instruction . . . .
–David Pearson

Assessment. Assessment should be ongoing and integral throughout the lesson since student performance is the best index for proceeding to each successive step of the lesson. Teachers who are constantly weighing student responses can adjust their instruction accordingly. Student mastery of the strategy or skill will be best measured by determining how well the student can use it independently when reading complete texts. However, "reading, like playing a musical instrument, is not something that is mastered once and for all at a certain age. Rather it is a skill that continues to improve through practice" (Anderson). Guidelines for helping teachers make instructional decisions about planning, teaching, and assessing a comprehension lesson are found in table 5.

Table 5 ▪

Guidelines for Making Instructional Decisions

Planning for Teaching

Text

1. What is the structure of the selection?
2. What are the theme(s), main idea(s) and major concepts of the selection?
3. What is the text-critical vocabulary?
4. What problems are there with the text that will interfere with comprehension?
5. What positive features of text will support comprehension?
6. What strategies and skills will be most helpful to students for comprehending the selection?

Reader

1. How can student background knowledge be assessed for the following?
   - Topic of text
   - Structure of text
   - Strategies and skills
   - Vocabulary
2. What are students' instructional levels?
3. What predictions can be made about students' interests and attitudes toward the topic of the text?
4. What predictions can be made about what students will see as the value of the assignment(s)?
5. How much teacher guidance will students require?

Context

- **Task**
  1. What will be the content objective(s)?
  2. Who will determine the content objectives? Teacher, students, or teacher and students together?
  3. What will be the reading strategy(ies) or skill(s) objective(s)?

Setting

- **Lesson context**
  1. How will I organize the components of the lesson to orchestrate my observations of text and reader?
  2. How will I organize the components of the lesson to lead to strategic behavior?
  3. What teaching procedures will I select to guide students toward strategic behavior?
  4. What steps will I build into the lesson so that I am gradually releasing responsibility for executing the strategy(ies) to the students so that they are evaluating, planning, monitoring, and regulating their comprehension?
  5. Should this lesson be part of a unit of instruction for the strategy, skill, or content?
  6. Have I included the minimum components for a lesson designed to read a selection?
     - Activation of background knowledge
     - Development of meaning of text critical vocabulary
     - Guidance of comprehension
  7. Am I developing a lesson using realisitic reading materials and purposes?
  8. How can I make the lesson interesting?
  9. What activities should I include for Teacher-guided Practice? Independent practice – narrow contexts, independent practice – wide contexts, informal evaluation?

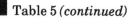 Table 5 *(continued)*

Guidelines for Making Instructional Decisions

Setting (continued)

- **Classroom context**
  How will I organize the classroom to best support learning for this lesson?

- **Curriculum context**
  1. How will I relate this lesson to past and future lessons designed to guide development of independent strategic behavior?
  2. How will I help students use the strategy(ies) and skill(s) learned in this lesson in other content areas?

Teaching

Presentations

1. Am I teaching rather than simply telling children to do things?
2. Am I using *modeling, explanation,* and *discovery* to teach the strategy(ies), skill(s) and content?
3. Have I made the usefulness of a strategy and skill clear to the students?
4. Am I focusing on getting meaning from text during the lesson?
5. Am I providing for active student involvement with text?
6. Am I consistently requiring the students to demonstrate their thinking process by telling how they arrived at answers to questions rather than just giving unsupported answers?
7. Am I consistently and informally evaluating student performance throughout the lesson and adjusting my instruction accordingly?

Teacher-Guided Practice

1. Am I gradually shifting my role from information giver to the role of coach who guides students to assume ownership of the strategy and skill?
2. Am I ensuring that students are practicing with success?
3. Am I ensuring that students are directing their attention to the task?
4. Am I challenging students to monitor their reading by asking themselves, "Does it make sense?"
5. Am I continuing with items 3-7 in "Presentation" above?

Optional - Isolated Contexts

1. Do I include isolated practice in lessons *only when necessary*?
2. Do I rapidly shift the practice to complete texts in narrow contexts?

Independent Practice - Narrow Contexts

1. Does the activity require students' focused practice on the lesson objective(s)?
2. Are the practice materials realistic reading materials?
3. Does the activity allow students to become more and more independent in the use of the strategy and/or skill?

Independent Practice - Wide Context

1. Am I providing guided opportunities for students to transfer and apply the strategy and skill to a wide range of realistic reading materials including content area materials?
2. Am I supporting the students' incorporation of the strategy and skill into their strategic behavior (analyzing, planning, monitoring, and regulating) by
    - encouraging them to share their thinking aloud
    - praising their efforts at self-correction
    - reflecting back students' ideas – "What I hear in your plan are the following steps . . ."
    - labeling students' behaviors – "You made a good inference"
    - asking clarifying questions in discussions – "You each have different answers. Let's hear the steps you each used."
3. Have I shifted my role so that students are now taking ownership for using the strategy and/or skill?

Assessment

Ongoing Assessment During the Lesson

1. Do students demonstrate their thinking aloud?
2. Do students understand and remember the content of the lesson?
3. Can students use the strategy and skill during independent practice?
4. Do students show evidence that they are ready to apply the strategy and skill in wider contexts?

Transfer/Application

1. Can students apply the strategy and skill in contexts different from initial instructional context?
2. Have students consciously and independently incorporated the strategy and/or skill into their strategic reading behavior – by analyzing, planning, monitoring, and regulating?
3. Do students demonstrate self-correcting behaviors?
4. Can students describe the problem-solving steps they are taking to obtain meaning from selections?
5. Do students try solving reading problems on their own before seeking my assistance?

Table 6

Basic Instructional Procedures for Teaching Comprehension

Three basic teaching procedures which can be used during the presentation step of the teaching cycle to introduce a variety of comprehension strategies are modeling, discovery, and direct explanation. Table 6 includes description of each procedure.

Modeling. Teacher demonstrates the strategy by thinking the steps aloud.

Presentation
1. Develop appropriate background knowledge and word meaning.
2. Demonstrate the strategy for the students by talking through how you would do it.
3. Give a summary explanation of what you did providing a definition of the strategy.

Teacher-Guided Practice
4. Ask student to do as you did with another example.
5. Provide opportunities for frequent student responses and reinforcement.
6. As students respond correctly, reduce the cues.
7. Practice with several examples as a group before asking students to apply the strategy.

Independent Practice - Narrow and Wide Contexts
8. Guide students to use the new strategy while reading in narrow and wide contexts.

Discovery. Teacher provides examples and guides the students to discover the process.

Presentation
1. Develop appropriate background knowledge and word meaning.
2. Provide an example and lead students to discover the process or principles involved in the strategy.
3. Ask questions which lead student to perform the strategy.
4. Have students explain what they are doing.
5. Provide frequent reinforcement by giving corrective feedback summarizing and naming what they have done.
6. As students begin to be able to do the strategy, gradually reduce the cues or questioning.
7. If responses are incorrect, continue highlighting and questioning until students can perform correctly.
8. Give verbal praise for correct responses.

Teacher-Guided Practice
9. Practice with several examples as a group before asking students to apply the strategy.
10. Guide students to use new strategy while reading Narrow and Wide Contexts.

Direct Explanation. Teacher tells students about what they will learn, then presents and explains an example.

Presentation
1. Develop appropriate background knowledge and word meaning.
2. Tell the students the objective of the lesson. Tell them what they are going to learn, how they will use it, and why and when it will be useful.
3. Present the example and tell them how the strategy works. This step is similar to modeling mentioned earlier since you will need to demonstrate some thinking aloud.

Teacher-Guided Practice
4. Provide more examples and guide the students to use the strategy.
5. The next steps are the same as 3-10 in the discovery procedure above which included Independent Practice – Narrow and Wide Contexts.

Making inferences is an integral part of constructing meaning from text because all of the information is not supplied in the text. The text provides clues to meaning, which, when used in conjunction with the reader's knowledge of the topic and the text, results in inferences. A good reader probably draws 100-200 inferences per page of text and readily uses inference in all reading. On the other hand, a poor reader is often not conscious of what to do when asked to make inferences. Many teachers have heard a poor reader say, "But it's not in the book!", when asked inferential questions.

Teaching an Inference Lesson

The sample lessons that follow illustrate not only how to present the concept of basic inference but also illustrate the three basic teaching procedures described in table 6. Because of space limitations, only the teaching cycle is included here. A classroom lesson should include all of the steps of the teaching cycle. During the planning step, teachers would consider text, task, and reader guidelines to be sure that the lesson is designed to best meet student needs. This planning would be followed by teaching, including presentation and teacher-guided practice. After the teaching step, teachers would provide appropriate practice activities in both narrow and wide contexts and then assess the outcome of instruction.

Sample Inference Lessons

Objective for all sample lessons. Students will be able to demonstrate and explain how to make simple inferences.

Definition. Basic inference includes combining in-the-head knowledge with on-the-page clues. In-the-head + on-the-page = inference. The basic procedure is the same whether teachers are asking students to make cause and effect inferences, predictions, conclusions, or inferences about character traits; state main ideas; or practice any of the many comprehension skills listed in teacher's manuals.

Instruction. The following short poem has been selected for this lesson. The procedures can be followed for any printed text and any grade level. Teachers simply select material to match students' abilities. It is important to teach inference skills at all stages.

Inference Lesson

What is it?*

By Charles Malam

The dinosaurs are not all dead.
I saw one raise its iron head
To watch me walking down the road
Beyond our house today.
Its jaws were dripping with a load
Of earth and grass that it had cropped
It must have heard me where I stopped,
Snorted white steam my way,
And stretched its long neck out to see,
And chewed, and grinned quite amiably.

Reprinted from: Reflections on a Gift of Watermelon Pickle

Making Inferences: Modeling

1. "What is a riddle? What do you have to do to solve a riddle?" After reading, discuss *cropped* and *amiably* as they come up in the context of the discussion.

2. "I have a poem that is like a riddle. How can I figure out what the poem is talking about? When something is a riddle, that means there are some clues to help me solve it. When I read, I'm going to have to look for clues. To solve this riddle, I'll have to use my head. I think I'll read the whole poem first to see what it's about." Teacher reads poem aloud with expression.

   • "Well, I have some ideas for what it could be about. Do you have some? Let's list our ideas on the board." Teacher lists ideas on board. Students might say dinosaurs, monsters, steam shovels. It is important to accept and affirm all responses.

   • "The next thing I have to do is list all of the clues in the poem about this unknown thing. You can help me. The first line is a clue that says, 'The dinosaurs are not all dead.' That must mean that the thing in the poem is in our world today and that it is something like a dinosaur. What do you think?" List clues on the board, and involve as many students as possible.

   • "I bet you are already fairly sure what this riddle is about, but let's check to be sure. The next thing I have to do is to compare the clues to the things I know about dinosaurs, monsters, and steam shovels. All of the clues must fit one of them, or I am going to have to do some more thinking. When all of the clues fit, I have solved the riddle. Let's do it together." Teacher discusses with students how well each clue fits the three guesses.

3. "Aha!! I just made an inference. I put together the clues I found in the poem with the information I had in my head about dinosaurs, monsters, and steam shovels to make an inference. Inferences = on-the-page clues + in-the-head knowledge."

4. Teacher displays another short poem. The children should have the background knowledge to work with it as a riddle. The teacher then guides the students through the procedure as described above. Note that this lesson would probably continue over a period of several days to include other steps of teaching cycle.

Making Inferences: Discovery

The difference between modeling and discovery is that the teacher does not "think out loud." The teacher's role is to guide the students to discover the procedure through careful questioning.

1. "What is a riddle? What do you have to do to solve a riddle?" After reading, discuss *cropped* and *amiably* as they come up in the context of the discussion.

2. "Here is a poem that is a riddle. What is it? I'll read so we can collect clues about what the poem could be about. Then you can tell me what you think is the answer to the riddle." Teacher displays and reads the poem with expression.

   ● "What do you think the poem is talking about?" Teacher writes all ideas on chalkboard.

3. "Let's see if we can figure out how you decided to make these guesses. What did you do?" Teacher guides students to describe the thinking process they used to get the answers.

   ● "How do we know which answer is best?" Teacher guides students to use clues to verify answers.

4. "What could you say in a few sentences that would describe the thinking you did to solve the riddle?" Answers from students are typically phrased in relationship to the example provided. Teacher guides students to identify that they drew upon the knowledge in their heads and used the clues in the poem to arrive at their answers.

5. The teacher summarizes and names the process. "You have been making inferences. Inferences are educated guesses. Inferences = knowledge in-my-head + clues on-the-page. You used the knowledge in your head about steam shovels and dinosaurs together with careful thinking about the clues on the page and made inferences."

6. Teacher provides a new example for which students have appropriate background knowledge and students proceed with steps above.

Making Inferences: Direct Explanation

1. "Today you are going to learn how you think when you make inferences. Making inferences requires a special kind of thinking that we do all of the time. To make inferences we put together the knowledge in our heads and clues we see, read, hear, smell, or touch. Since we are going to be making inferences in reading, we will look for the clues on the pages of our book. Inference = knowledge in-the-head + clues on-the-page. You are going to be using inference all day long in everything you study. You will need to make inferences to answer questions in reading, science, and social studies. You will use it to discuss stories and other topics. It is very important to learn about making inferences because you will have to make them all day long at school and home."

2. "What is a riddle? What do you have to do to solve a riddle?" After reading, discuss *cropped* and *amiably* as they come up in the context of the discussion.

3. "Here is a poem that is like a riddle. Let's see how we use inferences to help us solve the riddle. To answer our riddle we will have to make inferences. What two things are going to help us make the inferences?" Teacher guides students to state that the knowledge they have in their heads plus the clues on the page will help them solve the riddle.
   ● "I'll read the whole poem first. It will help to read it all the way through to get some general ideas about what it's about. Then we will go back and look for clues." Teacher reads poem with expression.
   ● "OK, I'll reread the poem and let's collect clues." Teacher reads poem, has students identify clues, and lists them on the board as they are identified.
   ● "Now let's think about those clues. What could all of these clues describe?" List all responses on the board. There may be only one response—the answer to the puzzle—steam shovel. On the other hand there may be several. All ideas should be recorded.
   ● "OK, let's check each of these inferences to see if they go with our in-the-head knowledge and the on-the-page clues." Teacher guides students to check the inferences against the clues.

4. Teacher provides another example within students' background of experience and completes the steps of the direct explanation procedure.

Making Inferences: Directed Reading Thinking Activity

Directed Reading Thinking Activity (DRTA) is another excellent strategy to get students to make inferences while reading. The role of the teacher is to guide students through selection in order for them to formulate questions for themselves, make predictions, and validate or reject the predictions. The strategy should be done over a period of time during which the teacher models and gradually reduces guidance until students begin to use the strategy independently. The final instructional objective is that the students should be able to independently apply the DRTA strategy to all their reading selections.

Steps

Activate background knowledge. "Look at the picture and the title on the first page of the selection. Think about what you already know about the topic of the selection. Let's share our ideas."

Predict. "What do you think the selection will be about? What do you think will happen next?"

Support the prediction. "Why do you think so?"

Read silently. The students read a section of the text such as an episode or episodes in a story.

Confirm or reject the predictions. "What predictions can you prove? Why or why not?"

Repeat the cycle. Use with the next section of the selection.

Many teachers find it useful to write predictions and modifications on the board to focus the discussion as they progress through the selection.

Planning for Content–Area Reading

The content-area teacher is in a good position to help students learn both the *content* of the course and the *processes* needed to become independent learners.

The first task for the teacher in preparing a lesson is to identify both the content and process objectives which are to be presented. This task requires the teacher to decide what is important for the student to know and what is the most effective way for the student to learn it.

Next, the teacher needs to select the materials and methods which are most effective for presenting the content. Some teachers have concluded that it is easier to present concepts entirely through lectures, worksheets, and media because the students have difficulty with reading. But this does not help students become independent learners. Instead, it increases their dependence on the teacher as a source for information and results in students who lack the study strategies necessary for independent learning.

Prior to reading, the teacher needs to assess the students' knowledge in order to select an appropriate method for introducing the concepts in the selection. If adequate preparation is provided, students will be ready to use knowledge gained from reading in a variety of classroom activities.

The idea that reading instruction and subject matter instruction should be integrated is an old one in education, but there is little indication that such integration occurs often in practice.
–Becoming a Nation of Readers

Guiding Strategic Behavior in Content Areas

The instructional framework for developing strategic readers found on page 22 highlights the important role of teachers in developing students' use of strategic behavior. These steps involve teachers modeling the behaviors of analyzing, planning, monitoring, and regulating reading and then guiding students to independently use the behaviors for learning from content-area reading. As the students take over the dominant role, teachers become moderators and coaches.

Guidelines for helping students develop strategic behavior as they learn from text is provided in table 7. The Directed Reading Thinking Activity (DRTA) described on page 96 has been modified to demonstrate the steps teachers model as they guide students in independent strategic behavior. The framework, which integrates specific reading strategies or processes into content reading while encouraging development of critical reading and thinking, is appropriate for all subject areas. The procedure involves analyzing, planning, monitoring, regulating, and reflecting.

Each step is described in the Framework for Guiding Strategic Behavior in Content Areas. The framework can be adapted to various content areas.

Framework for Guiding Strategic Behavior in Content Areas

Analyze: Preparing for Reading

Before giving a reading assignment, examine the reading selection or text to determine the features that would help student comprehension and identify unfamiliar vocabulary and concepts that might involve difficulties for the student. Next, assess the students' experiential backgrounds to decide whether they have the necessary concepts and vocabulary knowledge to achieve a satisfactory level of meaning from the text. If this background is insufficient, it will be necessary to decide how best to help students acquire it before they read the selection. Vocabulary instruction research indicates that a focus on concepts and meanings in familiar contexts is more profitable than a rote learning of new words in isolation. Unfamiliar vocabulary essential to understanding text material should be taught in rich contextual settings which are relevant and interesting. Vocabulary instruction should occur both before and during reading. The following are some specific suggestions for preparing students for reading.

● Assess and expand the students' background knowledge and experiences as related to the text or assignment by
  – direct questioning, to find what students know or believe they know;
  – noting misconceptions and offering information to provide adequate background for comprehension;
  – arousing interest and giving students an awareness of the relevancy of text material to their daily lives.
● Introduce necessary vocabulary and fundamental concepts by
  – brainstorming with students about the general meaning of new words;
  – guiding students to more specific meaning of new words in the assigned text;
  – analyzing the structure of the new words to aid in their recognition (roots, prefixes, suffixes);
  – developing a semantic map that links vocabulary to larger concepts.

Plan: Setting a Purpose

The more thoroughly teachers prepare students to identify the organization of the text, the more likely students are to achieve comprehension. Before reading a selection, have students preview it, examine its organization (such as headings, italicized words, summary statements), and develop predictions concerning content.

Through this procedure students identify a purpose for their reading. The teacher should focus students' attention on important concepts contained in the text. For example, a history teacher who wants students to understand the events leading to World War II should point out that a list of such factors may be derived from the reading. If geography or exact chronology is desired, that too should be made clear so that students have some sense of what aspects of the text material to focus upon. Some specific ways to help students set a purpose for their reading follow.

● Have students note the basic structure of the text, including introductions, headings, and conclusions or summaries.
● Discuss titles and subtitles in the assigned material.
● Direct attention to any graphic aids, maps, pictures, charts.
● Point out any study aids such as summary or discussion questions.
● Have students note new vocabulary which is highlighted (italics, bold print, marginal notes).
● Have students generate several questions of their own as guides during their silent reading.

Monitor: Guided Silent Reading

Once reading purposes are clearly in mind, students read the assigned material silently at their individual pace. Some ways of promoting effective silent reading follow.
- Have students create guides (questions, outline, chart) to refer to while reading.
- Guide students to create structured overviews of text material, focusing on identifying main ideas, key facts.

Discuss: Rereading

Following purposeful silent reading, students should be guided in the discussion of the reading content. Provide them an opportunity to talk about the content in relation to their purposes for reading it. They should discuss whether the information acquired was sufficient to answer their questions and fulfill expectations. Where relevant, they should describe how and why purposes for reading changed as they completed the assignment.

Reflect: Critical Thinking

During discussion, ask questions requiring students to go beyond the specific details and think critically about the overall concepts and longer messages in the text. Have them verify their reasons by rereading sections to support interpretations or to identify inconsistencies in the writer's reasoning. Rereading passages can be done either orally or silently, but should always be read with a definite purpose. Following are specific activities involving discussion, reading, and reflections.
- Discuss answers to prereading purpose questions, confirming and verifying answers.
- Interpret information from reading by drawing conclusions, making inferences, generalizing, and identifying interrelationships.
- Evaluate information by making judgments, determining writer's intent, comparing with other texts, and considering the overall significance of the information.
- Reflect upon information by applying to real life (local and current) situations.
- Identify topics from reading for further research analysis, discussion, and perhaps writing.

Apply: Extension Activities

Extension activities serve to help students expand upon information gained from the reading. Such activities provide students opportunities to incorporate new ideas and information into their background understanding. Below are some suggestions for extending ideas derived from critical reading.
- Create structured overviews of the central concepts.
- Locate and read additional information on one aspect of the material or topic.
- Relate material to a writing activity such as
  - writing a sentence using a key term from the text;
  - writing a framed paragraph;
  - summarizing or discussing the main ideas in exposition or narration (a brief story, an imaginary dialogue, a dream);
  - writing a newspaper editorial or article using the information.

Research has shown that strategies used for reading and learning depend upon the task and the text (Baker and Brown, 1984; Brown, 1980; Armbruster and Baker, in press). For example, if retention of information is the purpose, study strategies that allow students to organize the material and relate new information to what they already have would be appropriate. These strategies might include such activities as semantic mapping, structured overviews, note taking, and summarizing.

Recent researchers have identified effective strategies for dealing with different texts and varying tasks. These comprehension strategies first need to be taught and modeled by teachers who then guide students to use the strategies independently for comprehending and recalling information. In addition to modeling the *what* and *how*, teachers need to model *when* and *where* the strategy is appropriate and emphasize that text and task determine the strategy to be used.

The comprehension strategies outlined in this section are not intended to constitute an entire reading comprehension curriculum. Rather, they are intended to serve as prototype for the development of a range of comprehension strategies. It is important to keep in mind that all of these strategies are appropriate for a considerable range of difficulty and complexity and can be used throughout most stages by adapting the content (the text) and the task. Four comprehension strategies are described here.

Structured Overview

Description

A structured overview is a graphic depiction of the important vocabulary and concepts of a reading assignment or content unit. The overview, constructed so that important relationships between vocabulary and concepts can be clearly shown, serves to systematically introduce upcoming technical vocabulary and provides a mechanism permitting teachers to analyze what is important in the new material. The strategy is used initially as a readiness activity before the students encounter the new material and thus serves as a form of advance organizer. It may also be used periodically during the course of the unit to reinforce concepts and learning of vocabulary. New words or terms may be added to the diagram to make concepts clearer and to aid in the assimilation of new material. The structured overview thus provides a framework for students to learn the new material and master key vocabulary and for teachers to set lesson priorities and direct their teaching.

Procedure

1. Analyze the vocabulary of the learning task and list all words that relate to the major concepts you want the student to understand. Ask yourself which concepts are most central to the learning of the new material and then decide which vocabulary is necessary to understanding these concepts. Often difficult words which appear in a reading can be ignored because they do not directly relate to major concepts.

2. Arrange the list of words until you have a diagram (see figure 6) which shows the interrelationships with the relevant concepts.

3. Add vocabulary concepts which you believe are already understood by the students in order to relate the known with the new.

4. Evaluate the overview. Are the major relationships clear? Can the overview be simplified and still effectively communicate the important relationships?

5. When introducing the learning task, display the diagram and explain briefly to the students why you arranged the words as you did. Encourage the students to supply as much information as possible.

6. During the course of the learning task, relate new information to the structured overview as it seems appropriate.

Adapted from Cyrus F. Smith.

Figure 6

Structured Overview

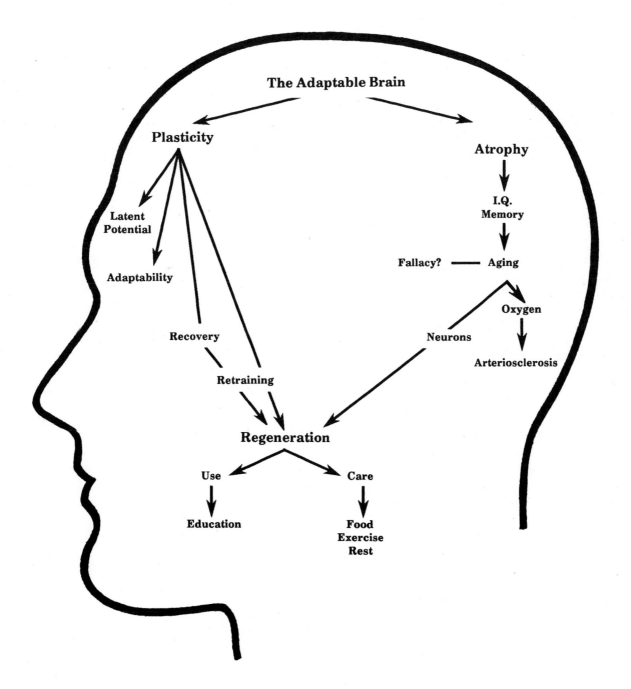

The Adaptable Brain

Plasticity — Atrophy

Latent Potential

Adaptability

Recovery

Retraining

Atrophy

I.Q. Memory

Fallacy? — Aging

Oxygen

Neurons

Arteriosclerosis

Regeneration

Use — Care

Education

Food
Exercise
Rest

Semantic Mapping

Description

Semantic mapping is a strategy for activating background knowledge about a topic or for encouraging vocabulary development.

Semantic maps (sometimes called conceptual maps or webbing) display words, ideas, or concepts in categories and indicate how words relate to one another or how they go together (figure 7). Such maps are valuable for students to link previous or old knowledge and words to a new idea or words and to see the relationships among words on the map (Johnson and Pearson).

Students are often helped by visualizing information learned from text. Semantic mapping is a successful method for helping students to see how information can be related. This information can include vocabulary concepts, main ideas and supporting details, or topics. Creating a semantic map has the advantage of total student involvement. Students are active participants in the process of developing visual maps of the concepts. Mapping can be an alternative to note taking or outlining. It forces students to read for key words and supporting ideas.

Procedure

1. Select a vocabulary concept or identify the major point of a reading and write it out on the board, or in the center of a piece of paper, and circle it.

2. Determine secondary categories or related words and write them around the central idea or word. Connect them with lines.

3. Identify supportive details and connect them to the secondary categories they support.

4. Be creative. Encourage students to use words, pictures, phrases, circles, squares, colors, whatever they feel best portray the concepts.

5. Discuss the ideas contained in the semantic map, and compare maps made by different students.

6. Use the maps both as prereading activities to activate prior knowledge and as a means of review and reinforcement. You can also use maps as a prewriting activity with main points on the map becoming topic sentences in paragraphs, and details becoming supportive sentences.

Figure 7

Semantic Mapping

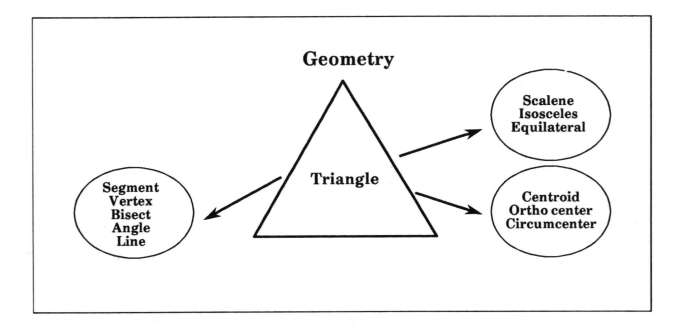

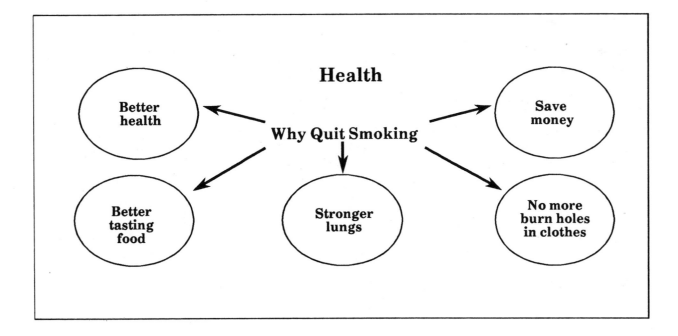

Questions-Answer Relationships (QAR)

Description

Question-Answer Relationship (QAR) is a framework for clarifying the different sources of information available for answering questions. The two basic sources are information in the text (*in the book*) and information from readers' background knowledge (*in my head*).

The strategy is effective for teachers to use in developing comprehension questions and for introducing organization of textbooks. The strategy is an effective tool for students to use in locating information, determining text structure and how it conveys information, and determining when inference is required.

The first step in using QAR is to focus on whether or not the information is *in-the-book* or *in-my-head*. When students have a clear picture of the differences between in-the-book and in-my-head and can make a distinction between the two, then each category should be further developed. Figure 8 shows the relationship of each category.

The in-the-book category is expanded to include two types of situations: (1) when the answer to a question is explicitly stated in the text, within a single sentence of the text *(Right There)* and (2) when the answer is available from the text, but requires the reader to put together information from different parts *(Think and Search)*.

The in-my-head category can also be divided into different types once students have a clear understanding that their background knowledge is a relevant source of information for answering questions. These two categories are Author and Me and On-My-Own. The key distinction that needs to be made here is whether or not the reader needs to read the text for the question to make sense. For example, the question "What do you think Jack might have done if he had not had the pail with him?" would not make any sense unless the reader knew why the pail had been important to the story. Here the answer must come from the reader's own knowledge base, but only in connection with information presented by the author. On the other hand, the question "What do you do when you are frightened, as Pat was in the story?" can be answered with information from the reader's knowledge base, even if the reader had not read or understood the story.

■ Figure 8

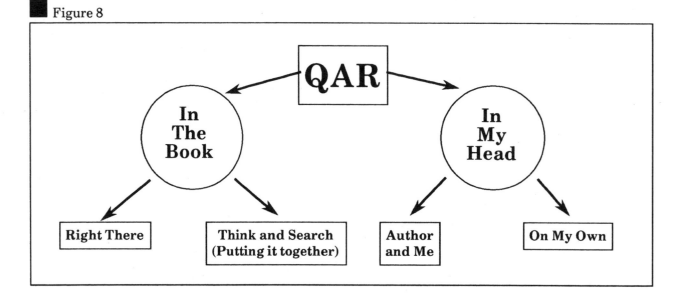

Procedure

Before Reading. Develop questions that help students think about what they already know and how it relates to the material to be read. Students can make predictions on their own (On My Own).

During Reading. Develop questions that will guide the students' reading. These questions should enhance the sense of the story content and should follow the structure of the text. Some of these questions will be from the *right there* category, but *think and search* questions should dominate because these questions require integrating information to make inferences and should lead to the asking of *author and me* questions (Right There, Think and Search, Author and Me).

After Reading. Develop questions that require student to think about their knowledge as it pertains to the text (Author and Me, On My Own).

Figure 9 presents a graphic illustration of the four types of QARs which can be used for overheads or bulletin boards to help students remember the key differences.

■ Figure 9

In the Book

Right There: The answer is in the text and easy to find. The words used to develop the question and to answer the question are RIGHT THERE in the same sentence.

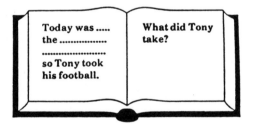

Think and Search *(Putting together)***:** The answer is in the story but you need to put together different parts of the story to find the answer. Words for the question and for the answer are not found in the same sentence. They come from different parts of the text.

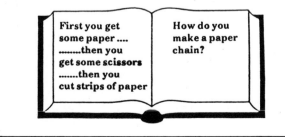

In My Head

Author and You: The answer is not in the text. You need to think about what you already know, what information the author provided in the text, and how it fits together.

On My Own: The answer is not in the text. You can even answer the question without reading the story. You need to use your own experiences.

Adapted from T. E. Raphael

Know-Want to Learn-Learn Interactive Strategy (K-W-L)

Description

In the K–W–L "reading to learn" process, elementary students learn how to learn from texts. This process involves students in three cognitive steps: assessing what we know, what we want to find out, and what we learned. Through a process of brainstorming, students call up what they know about a topic. Questions are raised about what we want to find out and are recorded. Teachers may ask students to find general categories of information by charting what they already know and by predicting how they think the text will be organized. After reading, students record what was learned and discuss questions that may not have been answered. Appendix F has a sample worksheet that is used to record the information.

Procedure

Discuss. Before students read, discuss with them what they already know about the topic of the article to be read. As students volunteer information, list on the board what they already know. An example of this would be an article on black widow spiders. Students might volunteer information about spiders, poison, hour-glass shaped markings, and spiders eating their mates.

Categorize. Ask students to find information that is related-pieces that are on the same topic or category. You may want to give them an example such as what black widows eat, where they live, or their mating habits. Then ask students to find other information that can be chunked.

Anticipated Structure. Ask students to think about the categories of information they would expect an article on this topic to cover. For example, explain that the article on spiders should include information about how that animal looks, what it eats, what enemies it has, and how it produces and raises offspring. List the expected categories on the board as students volunteer them.

Question. Ask students to use their own worksheets and write down any questions that have come to their minds as they read the article.

Learn. Suggest to students that as they read the article, they jot down answers to their questions on their worksheet. (Some may prefer to do this upon completion of the reading.)

Reflect. When students have completed the article and their worksheets, discuss what they learned from reading. Review their questions to find any that have not been dealt with satisfactorily. Suggest ways students could continue their search for information.

Adapted from Donna Ogle

Students need explicit instruction on how to comprehend different kinds of text and how to apply appropriate strategies for learning from text. Recent studies provide some general guidelines for effective instruction in reading comprehension (Jett-Simpson).

● Begin the lesson by connecting major selection content or theme with student background experiences, linking the known with the unknown (Marr and Gormley, Stevens).

● Encourage students to use background experience and text structure to predict what might happen in the selection (Hansen).

● Develop word meaning for unknown concepts central to the major theme of the selection (Vaughn, *et. al.*).

● Develop the lesson in the same sequence as events occur in the selection (Beck, Omanson, and McKeown, 1982).

● Provide *instruction* (explanation, demonstration, guided practice) before asking students to do the work independently. Don't be afraid to *teach* (Rosenshine).

● Ask questions that serve to *tie together important* parts of the selection (McConaughy).

● Ask higher level questions. Keep in mind that facts in isolation aren't as important as their contribution to the selection as a whole. Organize questions around the structure of the selection (Pearson).

● Encourage students to talk through *how* they arrived at their answers, giving supporting *evidence* from the selection. Such encouragement emphasizes both the *process* of solving the question problem as well as the *content* of the answer (Brown).

● Require students to *produce* answers rather than simply select from a list or multiple choice format. They need practice formulating their ideas into written and oral language, beginning in the upper primary grades (Wittrock).

● Guide students to use the structure of the selection as a basis for organizing their comprehension (Beck, *et. al.*; Fitzgerald).

● Guide comprehension in *all* appropriate subject areas.

● Guide students in developing independent strategies they can use to monitor their own comprehension (Paris, *et. al.*).

Organizing for Instruction   7

Grouping

Besides developing a K-12 reading curriculum, the district staff needs to address the way the reading curriculum will be organized for instruction. The traditional method of organizing reading groups within classrooms is usually done according to the reading level of the students. Ability grouping commonly uses the basal reader as the primary tool for instruction. The traditional three groups of reading instruction may help organize a classroom but have major disadvantages if used indiscriminately. Evidence from research indicates that static grouping patterns may be less effective than flexible grouping for specific purposes. Flexible grouping enables students to work with classmates of various abilities, with opportunities for the slow readers to model the reading behavior of the good readers.

The recent report, *Becoming A Nation of Readers,* noted that it is difficult with ability grouping for a child to move from one group to another within a year. Teachers are often concerned that all students complete all books or cover all material before moving to another group. In addition, teachers form groups at the beginning of the year partly on the basis of the children's standing the previous year, so changing groups from one year to the next is difficult. There is much evidence that keeping students in such groups diminishes achievement and affects attitudes.

Because of the serious problems inherent in ability grouping, the Commission on Reading recommends that educators explore other options for reading instruction. The recommendations include switching group assignments periodically, using criteria other than ability for group assignments, and increasing the time devoted to whole class instruction.

An alternative to ability grouping is to group by purposes. In a balanced reading program these purposes may include skill and strategy instruction, practice and application, and recreation. In addition to instructional reading level, factors to be considered when making group placement decisions are specific skill needs, motivation, attitude toward reading, rate of progress, learning style, and affective needs of students.

For some purposes, whether at the elementary, middle, or secondary level, instruction is most appropriately given to the whole class. For example, skills and strategies may be taught to a whole class, with reinforcement and practice occurring in smaller groups according to instructional reading level. This kind of grouping frees teachers to monitor and provide immediate feedback and assistance.

In the subject-area classrooms, many opportunities exist for flexibility and variety in grouping to encourage student involvement and discussion. Many motivational problems can be avoided if teachers will consider using various kinds of grouping. Groups may be formed to write informational reports, discuss contents of a favorite book, or share insights about the topic being studied. In addition, groups should be set up to allow for better students to model good reading behavior and motivation.

Table 8 ■

Minimum Allocated Instructional Time: Recommended by the Wisconsin Department of Public Instruction*

Grades K-6: minutes per week for a six-hour instructional day

Grade Level	K**	1	2	3	4	5	6
Reading/English Language Arts***	30%	700	700	600	600	500	425
Mathematics	10%	250	250	250	250	250	250
Social Studies	10%	125	150	175	200	225	250
Science	10%	100	100	150	150	175	250
Health	10%	75	75	100	100	125	125
Physical Education	10%	150	150	150	150	150	150
Art	10%	90	90	90	90	90	90
Music	10%	75	75	75	75	75	75
Foreign Language	---	---	---	---	---	100	100
Environmental Education****	****	****	****	****	****	****	****
Total Allocated Instructional Minutes		1565	1590	1590	1615	1690	1715

* While there is a recommended allocated instructional time for each subject, educators are encouraged to integrate subjects within the curriculum whenever possible.

** Up to one-third of each day in the kindergarten schedule may be reserved for students' self-selected instructional activities. The allocated instructional time recommendations presented in column K apply only to the portion of the schedule planned for teacher-directed activities. The time allocations for kindergarten are expressed in percentages to facilitate planning for various kindergarten schedules.

*** Instruction specifically designed to strengthen reading and writing abilities should be integrated with other disciplines, for example, health, science, and social studies. For further discussion of the recommendations, see *A Guide to Curriculum Planning in English Language Arts*.

**** Environmental topics should be infused into instructional units in all subjects, with the greatest emphasis in health, science, and social studies. A significant amount of time should be devoted to such topics. For a further discussion of this recommendation, see *A Guide to Curriculum Planning in Environmental Education*.

Time Allocations

Considerable attention has been given to time allocations, especially in the early years of schooling. Because reading is considered central to all learning, it has dominated the elementary school schedule. However, elementary daily schedules also need to include instruction in language arts, science, social studies, health, math, and other subjects. With a limited number of minutes in the school week and a great deal of instruction to be provided, teachers on all levels need to be creative in efforts to integrate reading instruction with other content areas. One way of making effective use of instructional time in the elementary grades is to combine the teaching of reading, which is one of the language arts, with instruction in the language arts. The guides to curriculum planning in reading and in language arts were developed with this recommendation in mind.

Instruction designed to promote students' learning from different texts and their abilities to respond to what they learn needs to be systematically included in all content areas. Table 8 provides some suggested time allocations for elementary grades. Users of the guide will want to refer to the general guide in curriculum planning and the content-area guides for further information.

Organizing for Comprehension Instruction

A number of comprehension strategies are mentioned in this guide. The generic reading lesson plans offered illustrate how to incorporate these strategies into the reading schedule. They easily can be adapted to any grade level, time schedule, basal reading program, or to a content area such as a science, social studies, or health. Four sample lesson plans designed for a 90-minute time block are shown on pages 115 to 119. They deal with the story mapping, background building, pattern stories, and semantic webbing. Teachers may adapt the plans to different grade levels by either simplifying or using them in a more sophisticated format.

Background Building

20 minutes – Brainstorming session	Entire class
20 minutes – Silent reading	All groups
30 minutes – Related activities	All groups
20 minutes – Teacher reads aloud	Entire class

Implementation

Background lessons are best used when a basal story lends itself to a theme that can be developed through experiences throughout the day or week or when a science, social studies, or health topic is being introduced. For example, if a basal reader contains a story about giants, the teacher might gather a variety of related reading material for both silent reading and reading aloud. A giant might be drawn on the chalkboard, chart, or overhead and children asked to tell what they know or think they know about giants. The teacher records the information by categories; for example, all comments about size would be recorded together. The vocabulary important for understanding or reading about the topic should be used to record ideas and to develop concepts.

Silent reading allows all groups to enjoy library and related materials. Library or trade books are excellent tools for prediction and inference practice. Independent silent reading provides a welcome change. The teacher moves around the room during silent reading, observing students and providing feedback or assistance or modeling silent reading. Drawing giants and recording ideas around the picture is a good way to summarize silent reading. Finally, the teacher reads a good giant story for sharing with the whole class.

Story Mapping

20 minutes – Teach story mapping	Entire class
15 minutes – Silent reading	Entire class
20 minutes – Present, discuss and compare stories Teacher records information on chalkboard	All groups
15 minutes – Independent work	All groups
20 minutes – Teacher reads aloud	Entire class

Refer to pages 41-42 and Appendix D for a description of story mapping.

Implementation

This lesson can be adapted to any grade level and time allotment. Use a familiar, well-structured story to teach the story-mapping strategy. Silent reading should occur in each basal reading group. Stories may be new or reread with the purpose of looking for story-mapping components. Younger students should do episodes at another reading session. During silent reading the teacher is moving around the class, keeping students on task, giving help and encouragement where needed.

During the discussion the teacher records information on chalkboard, chart paper, or overhead as each group presents and compares story-mapping elements.

	Group 1	Group 2	Group 3
Setting			
Main Character			
Problem			
Goal			
Solution			
Episodes			

Independent work may include assigning students to write a story, using story-mapping elements, or doing worksheets relating to the basal story. The practice materials may also be illustrations and labels of words, sentences, or phrases from story-mapping information.

Teachers should also read a story illustrating story mapping to the entire class. Students may make predictions, inferences, and observations while enjoying the story. The story can then be used by the entire group to review story-mapping structure during the next reading class.

Circle (Pattern) Stories

20 minutes – Brainstorming session	Entire class
20 minutes – Silent reading	All groups
30 minutes – Related activities	All groups
20 minutes – Teacher reads aloud	Entire class

Refer to Appendix G for an example of a circle story.

Circle (pattern) stories use a diagram to guide student comprehension, discussion, and writing of stories. This strategy follows a predictable pattern that students can learn to identify and duplicate. The main character(s) starts at one location and, after a series of adventures, returns to the starting point to live happily every after.

Implementation

Teacher reads aloud a circle story. The story is diagrammed to model this pattern. The teacher draws and writes as students offer suggestions. A circle with pre-shaped wedges representing the episodes may be used. Students then read circle stories (library books and basals are good sources for these stories). The teacher quietly moves about to check student progress. Students work in pairs (or threes) on a large sheet with a circle (a fine project for doing on the classroom floor). Students use scratch paper to briefly outline their episodes, thus organizing their information. Then they draw the episode in pie-shaped wedges. The final period is used to share efforts and enjoy each other's progress. This activity may take more than a single session. Circle pattern stories are great writing motivators, too.

Semantic Mapping (Webbing)

20 minutes – Teach semantic webbing	Entire class
15 Minutes – Silent reading	Entire class in own basals
25 Minutes – Develop individual semantic maps (web)	All groups
15 Minutes – Share webbing information	Entire class
15 Minutes – Teacher reads aloud	Entire class

Refer to page 104 for a description of semantic mapping (webbing)

Implementation

The strategy of semantic mapping is taught. Students then read silently from basals, text books, or library books. The teacher moves around room observing students (or may model silent reading). Students in each group have a teacher-prepared core question to consider in regard to their stories. Students develop individual semantic maps, using information from their own stories. Level of sophistication correlates to grade and ability levels. While students are developing maps, the teacher moves about class, giving encouragement and praise as appropriate.

When sufficient progress has been made, some students can share work with the entire class. Suggestions and discussion naturally follow. If more time is needed, the project can be picked up another day. Finally the teacher reads a good library book to the entire class. This book may be used as basis of a group semantic map the next day. Teacher models strategy on board as students volunteer story information. Several of these modeling sessions may be necessary before students learn this strategy.

Reading is one of the major vehicles for acquiring information in social studies, science, health, language arts, and other subject areas in which books or other print materials are used. There are many opportunities during the reading class and entire school day to integrate reading with these areas of studies. Students should be encouraged to apply the reading comprehension strategies taught during reading class; or the social studies, health, and other subject lessons should be used to teach the appropriate strategies. Independent application of strategies to all print material is the most important indication that students have acquired the strategies. Reading and writing are natural partners, and should be integrated throughout the curriculum. For example, individual writing should be a regular part of the reading and content-area class, with the following as possible activities.

- Writing answers to specific questions
- Writing summaries
- Writing original endings for stories
- Making notes about a main idea and supporting details, then organizing them into a well-formed paragraph with a topic sentence and supporting information
- Writing predictions about what may happen next and why
- Taking notes

Creative writing can also be included during a reading period, just as reading can be part of a creative writing period. Young people's literature includes many appealing stories to serve as models for writing in a variety of ways. First, the teacher or students read a story. The teachers may include a comprehension strategy such as story mapping at this time. Then, students use the story's organization as a basis for creating their own stories, or the group may work together to write a story. In order to create their stories, students have to demonstrate comprehension of the original story and its organization. In this way, reading comprehension provides a foundation for the creative writing.

*One aspect of every teacher's responsibility is to set up learning situations which will help pupils to use language as productively as possible.
–Allen, Brown, Yatvin*

Thematic Units

Another way to integrate subject-area curriculum with reading and writing is through thematic units. For example, the teacher organizes instruction around a topic of study such as dinosaurs, a traditional favorite among students. Science, social studies, reading strategies, language arts, mathematics, music, art, and most other areas of the school curriculum can be related to such a topic. This encourages cross-curricular use of skills and concepts which is an excellent way to unify curriculum material.

Envision a classroom involved in a dinosaur unit. A painted mural at the back, developed to scale, pictures different types of dinosaurs in their natural environment. Students would have researched necessary information for this by reading probably not only their science texts but also outside sources as well. Numerous fiction and nonfiction dinosaur books as well as books students have written, are displayed for classroom use. Original stories and poems which allowed students to practice related vocabulary and knowledge of story structure are seen throughout the room. The students will have learned a lot about dinosaurs as well as practicing and applying skills from different curriculum areas. The following is a general guide for developing a thematic unit.

● Select a topic from the science, social studies, health, or environmental curriculum, or a literature theme.

● Identify key concepts, vocabulary, and content to be learned.

● Identify reading comprehension strategies to be emphasized.

● Scrutinize overall curriculum to identify areas that will support the topic.

● Collect additional materials relevant to the topic that can be used on different curriculum areas.

● Develop lesson plans and collect and devise appropriate activities to carry out unit goals and objectives.

● Let imaginations of both teachers and students guide in developing further creative experiences and projects for the unit.

Integrating Language Arts and Reading

The following are components of an integrated reading/language arts program identified by one district. Also included is a discussion of considerations for classroom grouping. A detailed example of a weekly schedule incorporating these suggestions is offered in table 9.

Basal Groups. Basal readers offer a continuity of skills and a sequential order for the introduction of vocabulary, reading, and language activities. Three days a week can be scheduled for basal groups with the other two days devoted to individual or subject-area reading during which time skills and strategies introduced during basal groups can be reinforced and applied.

Class management of an integrated reading/language arts program is enhanced by constant reinforcement of skills. During basal group time, teachers should meet with each group to build background knowledge, set a purpose, develop vocabulary, provide guided story reading, and discuss the story being read. Students not meeting with the teacher can reinforce learned skills at a listening center, through seatwork, or by independent reading. There are several effective uses of a listening center to reinforce comprehension skills and develop listening skills. The following kinds of lessons can be taped for student use in the listening center.

- Basal stories or stories from literature or information books related to the topic discussed
- Lessons reviewing a skill previously taught
- Listening lessons encouraging students to focus attention effectively
- Language lessons reinforcing language skills

Seatwork activities promoting independence in reading and language arts include the following.

- Silent reading of the basal story or other appropriate reading material
- Writing answers to comprehension questions
- Writing predictions and summaries
- Practicing vocabulary and spelling words in a variety of writing activities
- Writing original stories or pursuing recreational reading.

Spelling and Handwriting. Spelling and handwriting activities can be combined. A good spelling program has students write words in original sentences or sentences dictated by the teacher. A strong, creative writing program reinforces spelling and writing skills and should be incorporated in every subject area at all levels. Students must continually apply these skills if the skills are to be generalized beyond a particular lesson.

Skills/Strategy Groups. Skill group time is an opportunity for the teacher to address the needs of individual students. Often when a new skill or strategy is introduced, entire class instruction is effective and time efficient. At other times the teacher can meet with small groups of students who need additional help or instruction in certain skills or who are ready to expand or extend their reading and writing skills. Students not meeting with the teacher may work in a group or individually on such activities as reading a favorite book or story, working on a project or a report, writing a story, preparing for a reading or language arts conference, or completing teacher-prepared application or practice activities.

Individualized Reading. Individualized reading is another way of providing flexibility in the reading instructional program. Generally, such reading in the classroom involves a variety of text materials for a wide range of reading levels and interests. Individual choice reading is an integral part of any comprehension reading program, reinforcing formal skills and promoting a general interest in reading.

Selection of materials may be based on student choice, recommendations of the teacher, or subject-area requirements. With self-selection reading, students choose books, discuss them with their peers, and complete related projects. This student involvement helps motivate young people to pursue reading.

Interest Groups. Students with a common reading interest may form groups to discuss their reading. Interest groups may be formed around a specific book, a series by the same writer, or a topic. The teacher facilitates the discussions, and activities such as plays and murals become opportunities for students to work cooperatively.

Story Time and Book Sharing. Students need to both read and be read to by their teachers. It is imperative at all levels that teachers spend some time each day reading to their students, and encouraging book sharing through a variety of experiences such as oral presentations, dramatics, discussions, creative writing, and art projects.

Scheduled Writing. Writing reinforces reading and language skills and offers opportunities for their application. While there should be opportunities for writing throughout the day, a time should be set aside for writing by all students. The teacher can use this time to meet with small groups of students to edit stories and reports while other students write and help each other edit.

Dictation and Proofreading. These activities enable teachers to assess their students' knowledge of language sounds, punctuation skills, and spelling. Proofreading helps students learn from their errors in a non-threatening way.

Table 9 ■

Weekly Schedule Integrating Reading and Language Arts Components

TIME	MONDAY	TUESDAY	WEDNESDAY	THURSDAY	FRIDAY
8:30-9:30	Meet with basal groups to • build background, • develop vocabulary, • provide for guided reading, and • discuss story. Other students may be at a tape station • listening to a taped story, • listening to a taped skill lesson, or • having a listening lesson. Still other students may be at their desks • writing answers to comprehension questions about their story, • reading their story or other books, • practicing reading or spelling words, • writing story summaries, • completing reading/language seatwork, • playing reading/language games, or • writing stories			Individualized reading program/ Conferences Provide opportunities for • free choice reading, • subject area reading from a variety of materials, and • individual conferences with teacher to make ongoing diagnosis.	
9:30-9:45	Listening Lesson	Spelling/Handwriting Activities			Spelling Test
9:45-10:00	Recess/Bathroom Break				
10:00-10:45	Reading/Language Skill Groups and Independent Activities Provide opportunities for flexible groups based on needs of individuals. Both whole group and small group instruction may be utilized. Skills that can be taught during this time include • word analysis, • comprehension strategies, • study skills, • language/grammar skills, • writing skills, • creative thinking skills, and • listening skills.				Scheduled Writing Time
10:45-11:00	Dictation and Proofreading/Peer activities				
11:00-11:30	Interest Groups/ Independent Reading	Language Activities		Weekly Reading (news time) or Subject-Area Reading	Book-Sharing Activities
11:30-11:40	Daily Storytime				

Secondary Reading Instruction

Reading traditionally has been isolated as a subject taught primarily in elementary grades and somewhat in middle schools. However, there is increasing evidence that reading instruction should continue beyond the elementary grades and should be incorporated into every content area (Herber, Early, and Sawyer). Even though Wisconsin statutes require a K-12 reading curriculum, a secondary program is lacking in many schools. A predominance of remedial classes exists despite research advising the contrary (Herber 1982).

Recommendations for providing reading instruction to all students at all grade levels are found throughout this guide. The comprehension model requires that reading instruction occur within subject areas utilizing textbooks and other written material. Furthermore, the development of strategic readers needs to be a goal of all content areas requiring reading for learning.

Content-area materials provide a rich source of reading materials for developing and practicing reading strategies needed for dealing with expository text. Students may be more motivated and interested in applying strategies if they are reading about Egypt in social studies or nutrition in health class.

K-12 reading curriculum includes teaching students how to learn from a text. The best place for this kind of instruction to occur is in the content-area classes with instruction focused on analyzing the text features, evaluating the task, and planning the appropriate strategies for comprehension. Each discipline has certain process skills and strategies which students need to learn to apply independently. Only through explicit instruction, modeling, guided practice, and opportunities for application can students develop as strategic learners.

Subject area teachers are in the best position to provide instruction that

- builds upon background knowledge about selected topics;
- prepares students for reading course-text material by analyzing task and text and setting purpose;
- models, guides, and applies appropriate strategies for reading text and related material;
- helps students monitor their own comprehension and make appropriate adjustments.

Providing for Special Populations

A major concern for any curriculum committee, especially in reading, is finding ways to meet the needs of special students. After the basic reading curriculum has been determined, it is essential to make the curriculum applicable to all students. The development of strategic reading behavior is important to all students and should be the basis for planning any special needs curriculum. The research on strategic reading behavior cited earlier emphasizes that strategic reading behavior is needed more by poor readers than good readers.

The Educationally Disadvantaged Reader

Educationally disadvantaged readers are those readers whose performances are below their potential. This group includes students found in a low reading groups, Chapter I programs, and execeptional education needs programs. Educators have considered many reasons for students' lack of achievement, ranging from economic or environmental deprivation to lack of language development and social/cultural differences to a lower level of cognitive ability. Current research indicates that differences in instruction have just as much impact on reading ability as variations in individual learning styles or aptitudes (Allington).

Good and poor readers differ in their reading ability as much because of differences in instruction as variations in individual learning styles or aptitudes. –Allington

In the past decade, reading research has moved away from determining what the disabled reader lacks. Instead the research has concentrated on identifying factors that affect reading achievement and pinpointing strategies that successful readers employ while reading. (Orasanu, 1985) This new focus has encouraged a positive approach to remediation and lends itself to the development of instructional techniques to help disabled readers acquire strategies used by efficient readers. The interactive nature of comprehension described in this guide encourages assessment which will determine the conditions under which a student can learn to read and progress in reading.

Instructional environment, or context, which includes teacher behavior, peer relationships, and classroom atmosphere, is of crucial importance in the implementation of the model presented in the guide. Significant findings demonstrate the importance of positive teacher-learner interaction in reading achievement. The scope and sequences in the guide provide models for teacher and student interaction. The suggestions offered throughout this guide to improve instruction are equally as important for poor readers and good readers. These recommendations include

● developing and activating students' background knowledge;
● providing direct instruction in how to comprehend;
● increasing the amount of silent reading time;
● reducing the amount of oral reading;
● providing daily opportunities for reading easy materials resulting in improved fluency;
● decreasing the amount of seatwork and workbook material;
● focusing instruction on developing readers who analyze, plan, monitor, and regulate their own reading performances.

Intellectually Gifted

The emphasis on higher level thinking advocated in this guide is most appropriate for teaching gifted students. Many ideas for challenging and motivating capable learners are provided in the scope and sequence for each of the instructional components. These students typically develop interests, abilities, and skills at an early age, show a precocious interest in stories and books, and are often self-taught in reading before entering school. A lock-step reading program seldom serves them well. While some of these students may not demonstrate the need for strategic reading behavior, such instruction should be provided as an alternative for approaching more complex, abstract reading and studying.

Careers and Reading

Students need to be aware of careers related to reading as well as the need for competence in reading for success in any career. They need to realize how important proficiency in all the language arts is to them as they enter the world of work.

Strategic reading is important in many careers. The models recommended in this guide for developing independent strategic reading behavior can help ensure competent readers who are able to perform effectively in a variety of work settings.

Reading and writing tasks in the workplace require being able to solve problems, read, and think critically. The K-12 reading program can support students in their development as thinking readers by focusing on critical reading at each stage of reading development and by providing many opportunities for reading a variety of materials.

Equity Considerations

The state and the nation recognize the difference in the experiences of women and men of all races, colors, ethnic groups, and of people of varied physical and mental abilities. These factors often result in the sorting, grouping, and tracking of minority, female, and disabled students in stereotyped patterns that prevent them from exploring all options and opportunities according to their individual talents and interests. The cost of bias to academic achievement, psychological and physical development, careers and family relationships is significant. Each student should have the opportunity to observe his or her own place in the curriculum, to grow and develop, and to attain identity.

In the development and implementation of reading programs and in the selection of materials, six forms of bias should be eliminated.

Invisibility. Underrepresentation of certain groups, which leads to the implication that these groups are of less value, importance, and significance.

Stereotyping. Assigning traditional and rigid roles or attributes to a group, thus limiting the abilities and potential of that group and denying students knowledge of the diversity, complexity, and variations of that group.

Imbalance/Selectivity. Presenting only one interpretation of an issue, situation or group; distorting reality and ignoring complex and differing viewpoints through selective presentation of materials.

Unreality. Presenting an unrealistic portrayal of history and of contemporary life experience.

Fragmentation/Isolation. Separating issues related to minorities and women from the main body of the text.

Linguistic Bias. Excluding the role and importance of females by constant use of the generic "he" and other sex-biased words.

Wisconsin school districts are urged to actively promote the value of all persons by including the contributions, images, and experiences of all groups in reading curriculum and classroom activities.

If we accept the premise that all people are special, we are better able to deal with individual differences in different individuals.
–Unknown

Selecting Instructional Materials   8

Introduction

There is reason to believe that instructional materials and quality of teaching in the early grades can significantly influence higher level achievement at high school and college. —Jeanne Chall (1983)

The literature on teachers as decision makers (Duffy, *et. al.*) points to the central role of instructional materials in influencing the activities of teachers and in establishing the content that students learn. Basal texts and their accompanying materials (teachers' manuals, workbooks, and related tests) have long dominated reading instruction. However, the research referred to in the bibliography cites shortcomings of many traditional texts used with students. Basal readers, workbooks, and textbooks have been criticized for the quality and organization of text, overemphasis on a scope and sequence of skills, a minimal amount of instructional procedures for teaching reading comprehension, and poorly constructed practice materials in the workbooks.

Basal readers and subject texts are certainly important components of a comprehensive reading program. However, their inadequacies point to the need for teachers to recognize that a variety of other reading materials helps to ensure effective reading development and learning in all subjects. Nontraditional materials such as magazines, newspapers, trade books, nonfiction and fiction books, poems, plays, and song lyrics are necessary to relate basal and subject texts to the environment and interests of young people. These materials should not only be readily available in classrooms and libraries or IMCs, but they should also be used in classes, small groups, and independent projects for reading and other subjects.

This section provides guidance for the selection of a variety of instructional reading materials. The other curriculum planning guides in this series also provide references for resources.

Basal Readers and Subject Textbooks

The first step in selecting basal readers, texts, and other instructional materials is to review the overall philosophy and program goals of the district. Second, develop specific techniques and procedures for selecting the materials which reflect the goals. Planners need to develop a clear set of criteria upon which to base evaluations of materials. The scope and sequence charts, section 4, will be useful in this effort, although each district should add or delete from them as needed.

If effective materials are to be purchased, it is critical for textbook selection committees to be knowledgeable about current research and ask informed questions. Local reading specialists can be most helpful in this regard. As has been mentioned several times in this guide and confirmed in the literature (Anderson, *et. al.*), the nature of textbooks and basal readers is being reconsidered. The Center for the Study of Reading has

130

been working with publishers to assure better quality in their products and has developed a series of pamphlets to guide committees in selecting new text materials. The first set of pamphlets focuses on basal reading programs; the second group deals with social studies and science texts. Guidelines are included for evaluating vocabulary instruction and comprehension instruction, and for analyzing workbook and supplementary materials.

The Center for the Study of Reading and the North Central Regional Educational Laboratory have information on the availability of these pamphlets. Addresses for both are found in the bibliography.

Supplementary Materials

If students are expected to read widely and frequently, a variety of books and other supplementary materials must be available in the classroom and in the school library. While basal texts and subject textbooks are useful in teaching students necessary skills and concepts, supplementary materials serve such other purposes as helping motivate less interested students, providing easier reading material for less able students, and offering additional insights on specific topics for all students.

Trade Books

Young people's trade books can add a dimension of fact or imagination to classroom texts in all subject areas and are available to match the reading levels of almost all students. Trade books are valuable supplements to assigned textbooks because they provide enjoyment, offer a means of escape or diversion from routine activities, stimulate students' imaginations, expand their understanding of language, and contain practical information about a wide range of subjects.

Subject-area trade books are appropriate at all levels. Their major function is to convey factual, non-imaginative material about the subject. However, an effective information book for young readers also teaches and stimulates students. The material should be clearly organized and expressed in a manner designed to initiate interest and guide comprehension. Well-written information books can fill a large gap in many reading programs by increasing students' background understanding and stimulating interest in various topics. Often they can effectively supplement, or even replace, poorly organized and written textbooks.

It is important to distinguish between books whose essential function is only to inform—including such reference works as an encyclopedia—and those intended to motivate and guide as well as to inform. The former often read like a shopping list of facts with little relating of topics and few efforts to stimulate reader interest. List-like presentations may frustrate comprehension among developing readers.

The preferable texts employ organizational, visual, and stylistic devices to aid in comprehension—progressing from material that is simple to complex, from concrete to abstract, and from known to unknown. They involve students in actively constructing text messages so there is a sense of collaboration between writer and reader.

Writers of good information books suggest activities to complement reading and ask rhetorical questions to encourage reader predictions. These writers are sensitive to the experience level of developing readers; they draw upon background understanding likely to exist among those using their books. Analogies, examples, and casual explanations are used to establish a bridge between readers and new facts and concepts. Technical vocabulary is introduced gradually. New words are incorporated with what students already know without confusing them. The unfamiliar vocabulary is surrounded by words known and comfortable to student readers. This consideration of the reader's background is known as *concept density*.

In summary, effective information books for young people are clearly organized, designed, and written in a stimulating manner; conceived to invite reader participation; are unambiguous as to purpose and progression of material, considerate of readers' background experiences, and sensitive to concept density.

Nonprint Materials

Nonprint material such as films, slide-tape kits, records and tapes, photographs and posters, maps and charts, models, and games can add a further dimension to facts and concepts gained from print material. Careful evaluation and selection of nonprint materials for both assigned and recreational use in a classroom or school library can enhance the reading curriculum. For example, a tape of professional actors dramatizing a short story that students have previously read serves to enhance comprehension and stimulates interest in literature. Maps or photographs of a remote country help students to visualize what they have read or will read in a social studies text.

The International Reading Association has a listing of specific considerations for evaluating potential nonprint material to be used in conjunction with a school reading program (see Appendix I). In addition, the association has itemized criteria for the utilization of this material in a reading curriculum.

The increase in the use of computers in elementary and secondary education has raised many questions about how computers can be most effectively utilized to further curriculum goals. The most successful use of computers to date has been for computer-managed instruction (CMI) to keep records, score tests, and prescribe what students should study. CMI proves helpful to teachers by relieving them of tedious and time-consuming record keeping, thus allowing them more time for guiding and instructing students.

The literature indicates that computer-based reading instruction will have an increasingly significant role in teaching reading. Until the present time, however, instruction has been limited by an inability to adapt the research on cognitive processes and curriculum design to computer applications.

In the same way that the new model for reading comprehension described in this guide evolved because of advances in cognitive psychology, it is expected that those advances will lead to a new model for computer-based reading instruction. Recent developments suggest that eventually capabilities of computers can be matched to needs of student readers in order to enhance learning. The versatility of computers makes their applications to the field of reading promising.

The International Reading Association has recently issued guidelines for utilization of the computer in the reading program. These guidelines are found in Appendix K of this guide.

Storylords: Computer Program for Reading Comprehension

An exciting program for improving reading comprehension in the primary grades, entitled *Storylords,* has been developed by the Wisconsin Educational Television Network. *Storylords* consists of twelve, 15-minute instructional video programs and twelve integrated computer programs. The video programs are designed to capture the attention of students through fantasy interwoven with reading comprehension strategies. These strategies are the same comprehension strategies addressed in this guide. Complementary computer programs allow students to review concepts from the video programs and through strategic simulation apply them to new situations. The program also includes a series of videotapes for training in teaching reading comprehension. Complete information about this program is found in Appendix J.

School Library

It was from my own early experience that I decided there was no use to which money could be applied so productive of good to boys and girls who have good within them and ability and ambition to develop it as the founding of a public library.
—Andrew Carnegie

The Library or the Instructional Media Center (IMC) is the best single source in the school to support and extend learning and to help develop reading. A school's library or IMC offers a rich variety of resources, including books and other media, physical space for individualized learning activities, and professional library media specialists.

Librarian. The most valuable part of a library media center is the librarian or the media center director. This individual should serve as a member of the reading curriculum committee. The librarian and the staff can work together to build a collection of supplementary materials to support the instructional program. They should also work together to plan an instructional program for students to learn how to use the library.

The librarian can provide book lists of the most popular and the best children's and adolescents' literature. Such lists are compiled and distributed by the Children's Book Council, the Cooperative Children's Book Center, and others. (See Appendix T for addresses of these sources of book lists.)

Supplementary Materials. A library has the supplementary materials listed in the reading development curriculum plus the most commonly used dictionaries, atlases, and encyclopedias. Other reference sources, such as periodical indexes and bibliographies should be available for readers at all levels. The library's card catalogue should be updated and used in teaching students where to find the material in various subjects.

Book Collections. The book collection should include fiction (adventure, romance, mysteries, science fiction), nonfiction works describing people and places, narratives of both ordinary and unusual events (sports, history, biography), how-to advice, humor, classic literature, science and nature, poetry and drama, and accounts of hobbies and collecting. A good library media center also includes captioned filmstrips, recordings of professionally read literature, and other print/audiovisual combinations.

Periodicals. Children's and young people's magazines available in today's school library media center run the gamut from preschool activity books to international news. Like the ever popular paperback, they draw children into the act of reading through attractive covers and illustrations. Their short, informative articles model good organization and concise expository style.

Software. The library or IMC is a good place to house computer software. Software allows for the individualization of learning and the involvement of students in learning activities.

The important feature of a library media center is the variety of the level, format, interest, and style of its resources. A well-stocked and professionally staffed library provides challenge and satisfaction, serving as a vital link between reading and pleasure.

Summary

Teachers need to become active decision makers in the selection of both basic and supplementary reading materials. They can seek the assistance of the librarian in building a collection of supplementary materials to support the instructional program. With the help of the reading specialist, they can examine basals, pick and choose the well constructed stories and accompanying materials, eliminate inappropriate or unnecessary activities, and refine the techniques for comprehension instruction. The same criteria should be applied for decision making about content-area textbook selection and use.

Evaluating the Reading Curriculum 9

Evaluation and Decision Making

Tests must be broad-gauged measures that reflect the ultimate goals of reading instruction.
–Becoming a Nation of Readers

A critical aspect of the curriculum development process is evaluation, the process of gathering information to determine the degree to which educational goals are being met.

Evaluation of a district's reading program should have three major purposes.
- To determine how well students are meeting program objectives
- To determine effectiveness of various components of reading curriculum
- To identify program needs and direction for change

The goal in evaluating any reading program should be the improvement of instruction; and if a reading program is to improve, it must change through decisions that are based on carefully gathered information. This information-gathering process needs to be ongoing to provide for continuous feedback.

An important distinction needs to be made between the process of evaluation and the subprocess of testing since they are often confused. Evaluation is the overall examination of relevant information in order to make decisions concerning a curriculum's effectiveness. Testing of a specific class or grade level is one of the ways information is collected; other ways might include teacher or student questionnaires, surveys of library usage, and recent alumni reading patterns.

Committee Role

In planning its evaluation, the reading committee is guided by the district's philosophy of reading. Assessment measures are selected by the committee to be consistent with the district's student reading goals and its definition of comprehension.

An evaluation plan will consist of the following steps.
- Determine purposes of evaluation.
- Review district philosophy and goals.
- Identify information needed and grade levels to be included.
- Establish a time-frame for collection of information.
- Select or develop assessment instruments.
- Administer instruments to targeted participants.
- Score instruments and analyze results.
- Decide upon strengths, weaknesses, and recommendations.
- Prepare and publish a report of results.
- Provide for short- and long-range planning for instructional improvement.

Built into the evaluation plan should be a system for involving teachers and community members.

An effective evaluation plan requires careful pre- and ongoing planning so that necessary and accurate information is collected throughout the school year. Included in table 10 is a detailed outline of the process district planners might want to follow in devising an evaluation plan appropriate to their purposes.

Evaluative information can be gathered from needs assessments, surveys, and staff interviews. Examples of techniques for assessing independent reading behavior include records of school and public library usage, district book fair sales, and observation of students' reading behavior during sustained silent reading time. An example of how one district evaluated a school reading break is included in Appendix L.

Annual Reading Program Evaluation Report

I. Purposes for reporting
    A. Required under Wisconsin law 118.015
    B. Provides an opportunity for administrators, teachers, and others to communicate needs and identify goals
    C. Keeps local school board informed about current features in the reading program (final decisions about the programs and staffing are made by the school board)
    D. Gives school board members opportunity to raise questions
    E. Enables school board members to communicate nature of the reading program to people in the community
    F. Demonstrates the importance of the district reading program as a priority worthy of school board time

II. Developing the report
    A. The K-12 reading specialist works with the K-12 reading steering (advisory) committee to decide on areas to focus upon (usually occurs September/October).
    B. Information is gathered throughout the school year and results are discussed in regularly scheduled steering committee meetings (4 per year unless other needs exist).
    C. The K-12 reading steering committee meets to determine items for the annual report and how it will be presented (May).
    D. Before the report's presentation, the K-12 reading specialist meets with the district superintendent to discuss items suggested by the steering committee for inclusion in the report (May/early June).

III. Presenting the report
    A. Explain briefly purposes for reporting, including the concept that program evaluation is a continuous process
    B. Explain briefly education context within which the reading program evaluation occurs
        1. Refer to philosophy and goals contained in the K-12 reading curriculum document, including focus on a balanced program (skill and strategy development, skill and strategy application, independent reading, and attitude development)
        2. Review the organization of the total program, describing the relationship of the developmental program and instruction for students with various reading needs
    C. Present examples of activities within various aspects of the reading program such as the following.
        1. Reports on book fairs where paperback books are sold to students
        2. Slides of parent volunteers working with students
        3. Slides of students presenting book-sharing projects to classes
        4. Data from high school student surveys regarding daily silent reading period
        5. Report from Chapter I coordinator concerning number of students served and describing some instructional activities
        6. Library circulation figures
        7. Slides of prereading instruction in subject area classrooms
        8. Art projects and other creative responses to reading
        9. Books written by students
    D. Present goals and major activities for the following year (staff development programs, curriculum development project)
    E. Describe long-term needs for reading program improvement.

Classroom evaluation is an ongoing activity that provides a basis for instructional planning and as such is an integral part of the district evaluation plan. By assessing student strengths and weaknesses, teachers can establish guidelines to assure maximum reading progress for each student.

Reading growth can be assessed through a variety of objective and subjective methods such as norm-referenced tests, criterion-referenced tests, teacher observation, review of daily work, teacher-made tests and checklists, and informal inventories. It should be emphasized that teacher judgment based upon daily observation and analysis of reading behaviors is a valid and most important evaluative instrument. Teacher-pupil conferences for listening to individual students read provide clues to their understanding of the content and use of reading strategies.

Through diagnostic assessment teachers can determine reading abilities of students and what they will need to enable them to progress. Not all students require identical amounts of instructional time, nor do they all need instruction in the same skills. An example of a teacher decision-making model for determining appropriate word analysis instruction is found in Appendix C. After strategies skills are taught, students need opportunities to practice and apply them. As they do so, teachers evaluate whether the strategy has been mastered or whether reteaching is necessary.

Management Systems

One cause of students' difficulties in reading has been the emphasis on teaching reading as a series of discrete skills isolated from each other and from the process of reading. Management systems were supposedly useful in identifying students' strengths and deficiencies in reading skills. However, their use sometimes leads to fragmented reading instruction with the parts becoming more important than the whole. In addition, many items on the skills list are too discrete, isolated, and boring to be significant as reading objectives in a K-12 reading program. It is the opinion of the task force that the new definition of reading comprehension as a dynamic, interactive process is incompatible with present management systems for reading.

Districtwide Testing

The Wisconsin Student Assessment System(WSAS) encompasses different methods of assessment to provide longitudinal information about student achievement that contributes to school evaluation and improvement. WSAS is based on three types of assessments: multiple choice and short answer knowledge and concept examinations, performance assessment, and portfolio assessment. Reading is included in the assessment content. Multiple choice and short answer concepts and knowledge testing of eight and tenth graders began in the 1993-94 school year. Administration of performance tasks to fourth, eighth, and tenth graders begins on a voluntary basis during the 1995-96 school year, with mandatory district participation scheduled for the 1996-97 school year.

Mastery tests must not treat reading as a set of discrete skills when research has indicated that a closely integrated set of processes supports fluent reading.
—Becoming a Nation of Readers

As part of the WSAS, Wisconsin requires school districts to administer the Third Grade Reading Test annually to determine level of reading proficiency. The test identifies the reading level of individual third-grade students with respect to a statewide performance standard; provides districts with information that will help them evaluate the effectiveness of their primary reading programs; and allows school districts to compare the performance of their students with state performance levels. For more information about the assessment program, contact the Office for Educational Accountability at the Wisconsin Department of Public Instruction.

It is likely that overemphasis on performance on skill mastery tests unbalances a reading program leading attention away from the integrated act of reading.
—Becoming a Nation of Readers

Use of Evaluation Results

District reading committees working with administrators should make extensive use of evaluation results in both short- and long-range planning. To gather information about the total program, districts often select one grade at each level (primary, middle, and secondary) for administering the assessment measures. As shown in figure 10, information gained at grades 3, 7, and 10 can assist in program development and improvement for grade levels above and below.

Figure 10

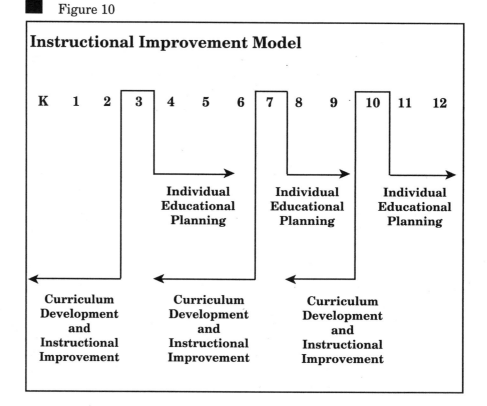

The following kinds of questions can be answered by a thorough examination and analysis of all assessment information.
- Has one component of the program been overemphasized at the expense of others?
- What information do classroom evaluation data provide?
- What components need to receive more emphasis than at the present?

- Does the present curriculum begin too early, or too late, to develop comprehension?
- Is there too much, or possibly too little, use of basal readers in the present program?
- Are students being motivated to read independently as well as to master skills and strategies?
- How well do students comprehend expository (content-area) material?

Assessment results should be helpful to teachers in planning individual instructional programs. If patterns of low performance occur at a certain stage or grade level, that aspect of the curriculum should be marked for immediate attention and alterations. Where low performance seems more a matter of certain individuals, the present program will need to be changed to meet their special needs.

Future Issues

Of particular concern for users of this guide is developing appropriate methods of measuring interactive comprehension to assure that students are advancing as strategic readers. In order to provide an accurate picture of curriculum effectiveness, assessments need to include evaluation of the reading process, understanding of reading purposes, employment of strategies, self-monitoring, and inferencing. The importance of prior information is a critical factor when assessing reading comprehension; otherwise students who simply review what they already know may be falsely viewed as demonstrating comprehension abilities (Johnston). The 1984 reading objectives identified by the National Assessment of Education Progress (NAEP) reflect comprehension as an interactive rather than reproductive process. The objectives also reflect an attempt to measure the reader's ability to use reading strategies. (A list of the NAEP objectives is found in Appendix M.)

Although the evaluation of reading comprehension seems to be lagging behind theories and practical suggestions for instruction, new process-based assessment models are being developed (Farr, *et. al.*; Johnston). Even though this guide went to press too soon to include new assessment instruments, that fact in itself is instructive. Advances in our understanding of how young people learn to read and improve their reading and what motivates them to keep reading and improving will continue to occur in the near future. It is the responsibility of all concerned to keep aware of these advancements in serving those young people and the future they represent.

These are not the last words on comprehension and instruction, but souvenirs of a journey that may entice future travelers to explore the territory themselves.
–J. Orasanu (1985)

Summary

The following steps summarize the process for evaluating the reading curriculum:

- Organize committee with broad representation (staff, administration, school board, community, students)
- Set priorities for evaluation goals that reflect district philosophy
- Identify criteria for measuring program effectiveness
- Identify specific grade levels or stages to be evaluated
- Develop and administer measurement instruments to teachers, students, administrators, and community
- Score instruments and analyze results
- Identify strengths and problem areas
- Analyze and discuss strengths and areas of need within the following categories:
  - Curriculum—goals, scope, and sequence patterns (stages)
  - Instruction—time, emphasis, organization, and materials
  - Student—strong and weak groups (Chapter I, gifted, specialized, migrant, and bilingual)
- Develop an action plan that includes short- and long-term goals for strengthening the reading program.

Contributors to an Effective Reading Program 10

Introduction

To insure a reading program that provides the best opportunities for developing mature, strategic readers, many people must be involved. Teachers, administrators, reading specialists, parents, librarians, auxiliary personnel, school board members, community members, and students all can help enrich reading curriculum. By involving these people, curriculum planners will foster among them a sense of ownership of the reading program and that is essential for its success.

Teacher

All classroom, subject, and special needs teachers are key contributors to a sound reading program. Their commitment is essential, and it can be fostered by involving them in program planning, implementation, and evaluation. An effective program provides instruction that enables students to become strategic readers. Instruction must be determined by what students already know and what they need to know. The teacher is the professional decision maker who makes determinations based on such factors as developmental stages, ability, motivation, and curricular guidelines. Students are constantly learning; it is the teacher's responsibility to stimulate, extend, and reinforce that learning through appropriately planned instruction.

To contribute to the reading program, teachers must create effective reading environments and model appropriate reading behaviors. This is accomplished by demonstrating reading strategies, reading aloud to students, providing silent reading time, encouraging student interaction, and communicating realistic student expectations.

To ensure that teachers remain vital contributors to the reading program, participation in inservice programs is essential. It is the school's responsibility as well as the teachers' to see that professional growth and effective instruction continue.

Reading Specialist

In a project directed by Rita Bean (*Reading Teacher*, 1983) on the role of the reading specialists in providing leadership for the development and implementation of a K-12 reading program, it was found that the specialist is most highly valued as a resource to teachers in providing inservice, demonstrating strategies, developing materials, arranging conferences, and guiding instruction.

This guide emphasizes the reading specialist's role in the curriculum process. The reading specialist should provide leadership to the reading committee and act as liaison between teachers and the administration, consulting with the administrators and being supportive of and helpful to the classroom teachers. By being accessible to the teachers and aware of their continuing practices and concerns, reading specialists will be in a good position to work with teachers and to provide leadership and direction for the total K-12 reading program.

Reading specialists may also spend time working directly with students. Some of their time with students could be videotaped to be used, for example, for teacher inservices. The reading specialist can also serve as a resource to parents and the community.

Librarian

Trade books, reference works, and periodicals are important in the development of well-rounded, mature readers. Therefore, it is important that students have access to a library or instructional media center (IMC) and the services of a librarian. Even though a school may have excellent library facilities and a high ratio of books per student, the library will only be as inviting as the librarian is warm and helpful. A librarian can be helpful by assisting in the selection of books, serving as a resource to teachers and parents, and being involved in school reading events. Examples of reading events that could be initiated by librarians (or shared with specialists, teachers, parents, and others) are reading contracts, read-a-thons, and school read-ins. Parents and other community members may provide assistance through organization of book fairs.

The librarian might conduct some reading class sessions in the library rather than in the classroom. This will help to reinforce the concept that reading is more than a school subject and that library materials are an integral part of the reading program.

Administrator

Administrators must know how and when to involve their staff in the reading program, and must place a high value on staff participation and decision making. In situations in which curriculum committee members have been fully involved, they are likely to be highly motivated in implementing the results.

Administrators should continue to learn as much as they can about the reading process even though they are not expected to be experts in reading. One good way to learn what is going on is through observation of classroom reading; that is also an excellent way to encourage an effective teaching program. These visits provide the opportunities for developing, understanding, and communication as well as improving credibility (especially if the administrator occasionally reads to students or presents a lesson while in the classroom). Frequent interaction with the staff is important if the administrator is to communicate the goals and objectives of the reading program to parents and others outside the school. An event such as parent night can provide the opportunity to explain the district's reading program and the important role of the parents in fostering young people's reading and language development.

Family

It may very well be true–and we suspect it is–that given words enough and time, virtually any person might learn to read by the lap method alone.
–James Moffett

The foundation for reading begins long before a child enters a child-care center, nursery school, or kindergarten. It begins at birth through the sounds of language in the environment. During the earliest stage of reading development, family members are the child's reading teachers and models. Research has demonstrated that parents, siblings, grand-parents, and others have a profound influence upon a child's success in reading, and thus it is crucial that family members take an active role in the child's reading development.

Schools should provide parents with information, materials, and support to work effectively with their children throughout their school careers. The school can promote special activities fostering parent involvement and support: volunteer programs, parent training sessions, reading motivation programs, newsletters, and orientation programs. Parents receiving assistance become more confident and involved, which in turn affects the attitudes and achievement of their children and helps to create valuable community-school relations.

School Board and Community

According to Wisconsin law, the school board is legally responsible to implement Section 118.015 of the statutes which requires employing a reading specialist, conducting a reading needs assessment, developing a K-12 reading program, and conducting an annual evaluation of the reading curriculum. Although it delegates the implementation tasks to the administration and teaching staff, the school board determines district goals and policies and provides for funding.

In return, school personnel are responsible for keeping the board appraised of the status of the reading program. This can be accomplished through periodic oral and written reports, newsletters, and school visitations. Since board approval is usually necessary if improvements are to be made, it is critical that board members be informed throughout the total process so that they will be able to make knowledgeable decisions concerning the curriculum, staffing, and budget.

Auxiliary Personnel

Most students require special assistance in their reading development at some point. Although many teachers in today's classrooms may not have enough time to provide necessary individual attention, a variety of auxiliary personnel can help. Trained people, under the supervision of a qualified teacher, can work with children needing individualized help. Such auxiliaries may be called aides, tutors, paraprofessionals, or classroom helpers; they may be students, parent or parent peers, or senior citizens. Depending on the school, they may receive compensation or volunteer their services. Whatever the title or status, auxiliary personnel are often vital contributors to the reading instructional team. Their effectiveness will depend upon the amount and quality of training provided to them.

Auxiliary personnel help a reading program by
- extending and reinforcing classroom learning experiences;
- improving students' self-concepts;
- assisting in non-instructional tasks;
- strengthening school-community relations.

Criteria for selecting auxiliary personnel should be similar to those used in selecting teachers. They must relate well to young people, and be reliable and responsible.

Student

The single most important contributor to a sound reading program is the student. Accomplishing the goal of creating mature, strategic readers demands that all program decisions be made in relation to the student as learner. Curriculum should be student-centered, not content-centered.

Schools have the responsibility of providing students with the best possible reading program; students have the responsibility of interacting with the program to become independent strategic readers. Only when students assume responsibilities and understand their own cognitive processes are they able to control their learning. It is the task of teachers and parents to assist them in developing this understanding.

Appendixes 11

The Strategic Reader*

Analyzes

- Understands how different reading goals and various kinds of texts require particular strategies

- Identifies task and sets purpose (discriminates between reading to study for a test and reading for pleasure)

Plans

- Chooses appropriate strategies for the reading situation
    - Rereading, skimming, summarizing
    - Paraphrasing, predicting
    - Looking for important ideas
    - Testing understanding
    - Identifying pattern of text
    - Sequencing the events
    - Looking for relationships
    - Reading ahead for clarification
    - Mentally executing the directions
    - Relating new knowledge to prior knowledge
    - Summarizing
    - Questioning
    - Clarifying
    - Predicting

Monitors

- Monitors comprehension which involves
    - Knowing *that* comprehension is occurring
    - Knowing *what* is being comprehended
    - Knowing *how* to repair/fix-up comprehension

Regulates

- Develops a positive attitude toward reading

Reflects

- Reflects upon task at completion
    - Reflects on what is read
    - Remembers
    - Develops a positive attitude toward reading

*Adapted from Scott G. Paris, Marjorie Y. Lipson and Karen K. Wixson. "Becoming a Strategic Reader." *Contemporary Educational Psychology* 8 (1983).

Poster for Word Meaning Strategies

A Decision-Making Guide for
Teaching Word Analysis *

The maximum amount of instruction in word analysis should be the minimum amount students need to assist them in developing independent word pronunciation strategies. This is not the same amount for all students. Students who already use a skill for reading continuous text do not need instruction for that skill. For example, students who can fluently read consonant-vowel-consonant words containing short /a/ and can use that knowledge to figure out new short /a/ words do not need instruction for that phonics skill. Interestingly, many students are able to analyze words without direct instruction. They have simply developed their own problem-solving procedures. On the other hand, there are students who don't have a system for word analysis and need some instruction to help them develop one.

The purpose of the flow chart (see page 156) is to guide teachers in making decisions about what skills to teach and where to begin teaching in an instructional sequence. The oval shapes on the chart represent decision points and the boxes contain teaching sequences. A yes answer to a decision leads to a teaching sequence. A no answer leads to another decision-making point.

The first question teachers can ask themselves is, "Do the students already use this skill effectively when reading the basal reader and other materials - at the *story level*?" Teachers can answer the question by listening to students' oral reading. It is important to observe what students can pronounce as well as what gives them difficulty. A yes answer means students are reading new words that contain the skill element. The teaching decision is that no teaching is necessary. A no answer, shown by repeated patterns in the student's oral reading miscues, can indicate areas that may need teaching. A random pattern of miscues may mean the students simply need help in becoming more effective contextual readers as opposed to needing phonics instruction.

If the students are not using the skill at the story level, the next step is to assess to see if students can do the skill at the Word Level. How well students do on criterion referenced tests, worksheets, and teacher-made tests can be a source of this information. A number of students do very well on their worksheets but do not use the skill in the context of reading. Skills are taught to help the students build a network of clues they can use on their own to pronounce words when reading text. "Yes, students can do the worksheets for skills in isolation" tells teachers that their instruction should guide students to apply the skill at the story level. In this procedure, guide students to use an integrated word analysis procedure which includes
- reading the rest of the sentence;
- looking at the word parts;
- trying to say the word to see if it makes sense;
- trying again if it doesn't make sense; and
- if all else fails, asking the teacher or using the dictionary.

If the students fail the word level assessment the teacher needs to assess students' abilities at the **discrimination level**. This is the level where the teacher observes if the student can visually identify the letter or spelling pattern, auditorily identify the sound, and do sound/symbol matching. A yes to the discrimination level says that the students are ready to receive instruction at the **word level**. There are a variety of different word analysis approaches teachers can choose to use to teach at the word level including a model word approach, a generalization or rule approach, a whole word comparison approach, a family method, sound blending, and root/affix analysis. Teachers' choices should be governed by the type of skill under question and learning patterns of the students.

A no to **discrimination level** may mean that some instruction in discrimination is necessary. There are some students who have difficulties with auditory discrimination of sounds or letters; for example, dialect speaking students may have trouble discriminating vowel sounds. When their contextual reading is carefully observed, however, they are found to be effective users of that sound/symbol correspondence. So it may be that visual, auditory and auditory-visual matching are useful topics for instruction for some students and not others. It may be a better choice in some cases to bypass discrimination instruction and begin with the word level. Teachers also make choices about what instructional approach to use to teach discrimination. Some subscribe to the view that sounds should not be isolated for instruction so they will use a whole word approach to developing discrimination abilities. For example, these teachers would ask students a question such as "What words start like bug? pat? do? bat?" Others take the position that sound/symbol correspondence should be isolated. They are likely to ask questions such as "Which words begin with the /t/ sound? tap? run? jump?"

By making sound decisions about where to begin instruction, teachers can gain instructional time because they are likely to eliminate a good part of unnecessary instruction. They can also build successful lessons based on the background knowledge students have acquired on their own about word analysis. Teachers' knowledge of the variety of instructional procedures for teaching at the word level and discrimination level will give them flexibility in teaching instead of being limited to the procedures presented in their basal text manuals. Frank May, in *Reading as Communication*, Chapters 3 and 4, discusses the strengths and limitations of the different instructional approaches to teaching at the word and discrimination levels.

*Adapted from Mary Jett-Simpson (1984)

References

Durkin, Dolores. *Strategies in Identifying Words*. Allyn and Bacon, 1981.
Johnson, Dale and David Pearson. *Teaching Reading Vocabulary*. Holt, Rinehart and Winston, 1984.
May, Frank. *Reading as Communication*. Charles E. Merrill, 1982.

A Decision-Making Guide for Teaching Word Analysis

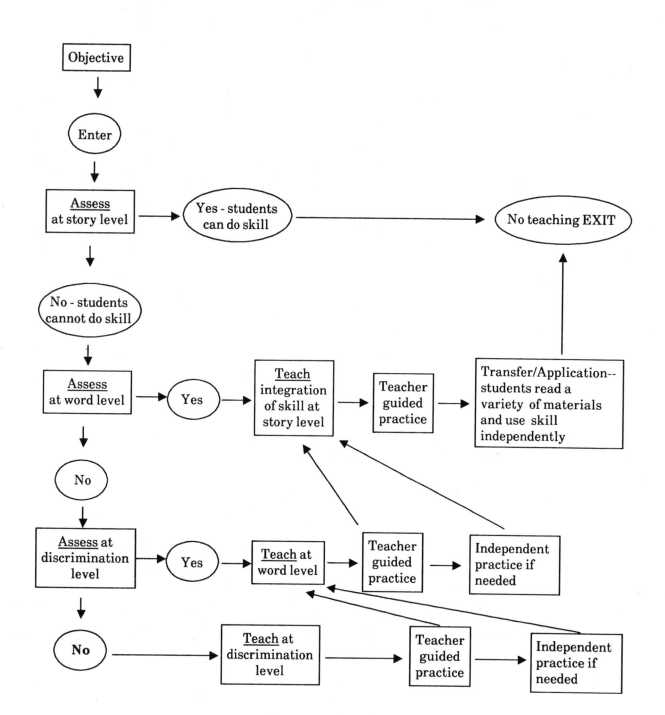

Story Map for "The Three Billy Goats Gruff"

Setting – on a hillside during the day

Main Characters – the three Billy Goats Gruff

Goal – to get to the hillside to make themselves fat

Problem – the troll who wants to gobble them up

Episodes – 1. **Beginning** – first goat starts across bridge
Development – troll says he will eat him but goat says to wait for the next bigger goat
Outcome – goat gets across the bridge

2. **Beginning** – second goat starts across bridge
Development – troll says he will eat him but goat says to wait for the next bigger goat
Outcome – goat gets across the bridge

3. **Beginning** – third goat starts across bridge
Development – troll says he will eat him but goat butted and speared the troll with his horns
Outcome – goat gets across the bridge

Resolution – goats reach hillside and get fat by eating grass.

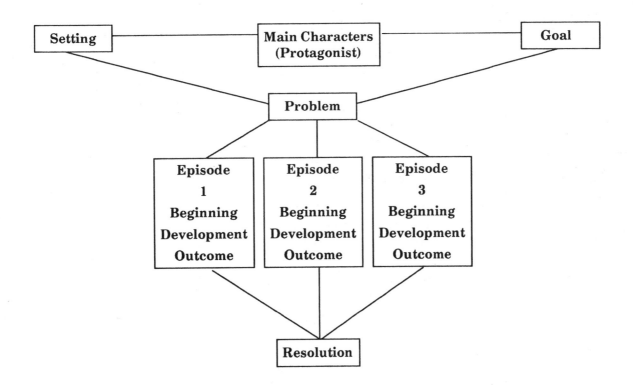

Model for Teaching Students to Summarize Text

1. Start simply. Use easy material.

2. Provide direct instruction (i.e. teach students how to summarize). The following six steps have been used in research* with students of various ages.

    Step 1. Delete trivial material.

    Step 2. Delete material that is important but redundant.

    Step 3. Substitute a superordinate term for a list of items or actions. If the text has a list of animals (cats, dogs, goldfish, gerbils, parrots), substitute the term "pets."

    Step 4. Similarly, substitute a superordinate action as "John went to London," for a list of subcomponents of that action, for example, "John left the house; John bought a ticket."

    Step 5. Select a topic sentence for each paragraph.

    Step 6. If there isn't a topic sentence, invent your own.

3. Provide feedback about the reader's effectiveness of summarization.

4. Provide direct instruction about *where* and *when* to use the strategy.

5. Provide training, lots of practice in many types of materials (stories, different content subjects of varying lengths and complexity).

*Brown, Ann, Joseph Campione, and Jeanne Day. "Learning to Learn: On Training Students to Learn From Texts." *Technical Report 189*. Center for the Study of Reading. Champaign, IL 61820.

K–W–L Strategy Sheet

What We Know	What We Want To Find Out	What We Learn – Still Need to Learn
1.		

2. Categories of Information We Expect to Use

   A.

   B.

   C.

   D.

   E.

   F.

   G.

Circle Story Diagram of "The Runaway Bunny"

Circle stories capitalize on visual diagrams to guide students' comprehension, discussion, and writing of their own stories (Jett-Simpson, 1981). This strategy follows a predictable pattern that students can learn to identify and duplicate. The main character starts at one location and, after a series of adventures, returns to the starting point to live happily ever after. Stories like Sawyer's *Journey Cake Ho*, Gag's *Millions of Cats*, and Brown's *The Runaway Bunny*, are examples of this circular pattern.

To teach this strategy, draw a large circle on the board or butcher paper and divide it into as many pie shaped parts as there are adventures in the chosen story. At the top of the circle, a house is drawn to represent the beginning and ending of the character's journey, whether that place is "home," the cabin of the journey cake, or Mother Rabbit's lap.

Read the story aloud and have the class recall the story to decide the sequence of events that need to be pictured in the circle diagram. For example, the figure below depicts the sequence of adventures in *The Runaway Bunny* based on a class discussion of story events.

The circle story strategy can be extended for small group work. Each group is given a story to diagram on large paper. Each student in every group is given a portion to illustrate in order to complete the whole diagram. Using large paper for this process allows students in each group to draw pictures simultaneously, an activity that motivates a great deal of oral language. Some students will want to label pictures while others may write descriptive sentences or even include written quotations for their character as the activity progresses. Sharing the finished products increases opportunities for language, reinforces the story pattern, and above all adds to the fun of reading.

Teachers will recognize the success of this strategy when students can use this pattern independently as they write their own original stories. Equally satisfying is the spontaneous recognition of the circle story pattern weeks later when a new book or a story is read.

References

Jett-Simpson, M. "Writing Stories Using Model Structures: The Circle Story." *Language Arts* 58 (1981).

Synthesis of Research on Staff Development
For Effective Teaching

1. Select content that has been verified by research to improve student achievement.

2. Create a context of acceptance by involving teachers in decision making and providing administrative support.

3. Conduct training sessions (more than one) two or three weeks apart.

4. Include presentation, demonstration, practice, and feedback as workshop activities.

5. During training sessions, provide opportunities for small-group discussions of the application of new practices and sharing of ideas and concerns about effective instruction.

6. Between workshops, encourage teachers to visit each others' classrooms, preferably with a simple, objective, student-centered observation instrument. Provide opportunities for discussions of the observation.

7. Develop in teachers a philosophical acceptance of the new practices by presenting research and a rationale for the effectiveness of the techniques. Allow teachers to express doubts about or objections to the recommended methods in the small group. Let the other teachers convince the resisting teacher of the usefulness of the practices through "testimonies" of their use and effectiveness.

8. Lower teachers' perception of the cost of adopting a new practice through detailed discussions of the "nuts and bolts" of using the technique and teacher sharing of experiences with the technique.

9. Help teachers grow in their self-confidence and competence by encouraging them to try only one or two new practices after each workshop. Diagnosis of teacher strengths and weaknessess can help the trainer suggest changes that are likely to be successful—and, thus, reinforce future efforts to change.

10. For teaching practices that require very complex thinking skills, plan to take more time, provide more practice, and consider activities that develop conceptual flexibility.

*From Georgia Mohlman Sparks. "Synthesis of Research of Staff Development for Effective Teaching." *Educational Leadership* (November, 1983).

Nonprint Media for a Reading Curriculum*

Criteria for Selection of Nonprint Media

Print media include printed material in book, pamphlet, magazine, or newspaper form. Nonprint media include any other means of conveying information, including television, radio, computers, music, games, audiotape, film, videodisc, videotape, and cable TV.

1. Materials should support and be consistent with general educational goals of the school district.

2. Materials should contribute to specific objectives of the instructional program.

3. Materials should be appropriate for the age, social and emotional development, and interests of students.

4. Materials should present a reasonable balance of opposing sides toward controversial issues, so that students may practice critical reading and thinking. When no opposing side of an issue is currently available, this limitation should be explained and discussed with students.

5. Materials should provide a background of information that enables pupils to make informed judgments in their daily lives.

6. Materials should provide a stimulus for creative reading, writing, listening, and thinking.

7. Materials should reflect the pluralistic character and culture of the students' society. They should foster equal respect of all gender, racial, religious, cultural, and economic groups.

8. Materials should have acceptable technical quality such as clear narration, synchronized pictures and sound, distinct images, and logical organization.

9. Materials should be evaluated for their aesthetic quality, to help provide students with an appreciation of their society and the world beyond, with a curiosity and respect for the past and future as well as the present.

10. Materials should encourage effective responses and further humanistic values and concerns.

Criteria for Utilization of Nonprint Media

1. Teachers should be fully trained in using audio-visual equipment before operating it in the classroom.

*Adapted from International Reading Association (Newark, Delaware)

2. Nonprint media should be ready to operate prior to scheduled use to avoid loss of valuable classroom instructional time. Room facilities should be considered in advance—electrical outlets, adaptors, seating, extension cords.

3. Materials should be previewed before utilization in the reading curriculum. Background information, including new vocabulary and concepts, should be provided to students to support concepts to be learned.

4. Prior to use of nonprint materials, specific goals and purposes should be discussed to help students identify expectations of the learning activity.

5. Content of materials should be discussed after presentation, and student understanding evaluated to assure successful learning of information and concepts.

6. Non-print media should be used in a manner to stimulate students toward an expansion of literacy and lifelong ability and interest in reading.

Storylords

Video: Norbert helps the good Storylord Lexor overcome the evil of Thorzuul who wants to enslave the inhabitants of Mojuste. Watch Norbert, the apprentice storylord, foil Thorzuul with good reading skills in this series of twelve 15-minute instructional video programs. These programs capture second and third graders' attention through fantasy interwoven with reading-comprehension strategies designed to help them better understand print materials.

Computer Software: Twelve integrated computer programs complement this new series from the Wisconsin Education Television Network (WETN). These parallel computer disks allow students to review concepts from the video programs and apply them to new situations through strategic simulation. A teacher manual accompanies both the video and the computer components.

Contents: Areas covered by the *Storylords* materials include
- prior knowledge
- basic inference
- directed reading-thinking activity
- question-answer relationships
- decoding in context
- story structure
- main idea
- pronoun anaphora
- independent reading

Teaching Reading Comprehension

Video Inservice: Fourteen 30-minute instructional videos help teachers and reading supervisors improve their knowledge of reading comprehension at the first through fourth-grade level. Using experts in the field, the programs show teachers how to incorporate reading comprehension lessons into their classes through *Storylords* or other materials.

Hosts Dr. Mary Jett-Simpson and Dr. Sandra Dahl introduce each lesson's concept, highlight the visiting specialist, and demonstrate through classroom examples how to incorporate the lesson in the class. The series focuses on the most recent developments in reading comprehension research and gives practical suggestions for direct classroom application.

Contents: Programs focus on the following topics.
- What's the Fuss about Reading Comprehension?
- What is Reading Comprehension?
- Language Experience in Communication
- Preparation for Reading (word meaning)
- Basic Inference
- Preparation for Reading (Semantic Mapping)
- Directed Reading and Thinking Activities

- Story Structure
- Main Idea
- Anaphora
- Individual Seat Work
- Guiding Independent Reading
- Questions and Text
- Comprehension and Decoding

Project Background: Both projects are funded jointly by the Wisconsin Educational Television Network and the U.S. Department of Education. Consultants are Dr. Sandra Dahl, writer of professional reading materials; Dr. Mary Jett-Simpson, reading expert from the UW-Milwaukee; and Doris M. Cook, reading education Supervisor at the Wisconsin Department of Public Instruction. Dr. Thomas DeRose, manager of program development for the Educative Services of WETN, is project manager. Evaluation was conducted by Dr. Margaret J. Wilsman, manager of research and evaluation for the Educative Services Division of WETN.

How to Order

Storylords and *Teaching Reading Comprehension* instructional components may be ordered from Wisconsin Educational Communications Board, 3319 West Beltline Highway, Madison, WI 53713-2899. For further information on ordering and costs contact Linda Hanson at (608) 264-9688.

These are the various *Storylords* products: *Storylords* video teacher guide(s): *Storylords* computer software (includes 12 *Storylords* computer disks; computer user guide; and *Storylords* video teacher guide) (Apple IIe, 64 format only) *Teaching Reading Comprehension* Video viewer guide(s).

Videotaping Rights

Programs may be videotaped and used in the classroom as long as the series is broadcast on the Wisconsin Educational Television Network. Copies of programs will be available from the Networks' Tape Dubbing service. Call (608) 264-9701 for information on dubbing costs.

Guidelines for Using Computers in a Reading Curriculum*

1. About software

Curricular needs should be primary in the selection of reading instructional software. Above all, software designed for use in the reading classroom must be consistent with what research and practice have shown to be important in the process of learning to read or reading to learn. The International Reading Association (IRA) believes that high quality instructional software should incorporate the following elements:

- clearly stated and implemented instructional objectives;
- learning to read and reading-to-learn activities which are consistent with established reading theory and practice;
- lesson activities which are most effectively and efficiently done through the application of computer technology and are not merely replications of activities which could be better done with traditional means;
- prompts and screen instructions to the student which are simple, direct and easier than the learning activity to be done;
- prompts, screen instructions, and reading texts which are at a readability level appropriate to the needs of the learner;
- documentation and instructions which are clear and unambiguous, assuming a minimum of prior knowledge about computer use;
- screen displays which have clear and legible print with appropriate margins and between-line spacing;
- documentation and screen displays which are grammatically correct, factually correct, and which have been thoroughly proofed for spelling errors;
- a record keeping or information management element for the benefit of both the teacher and the learner, where appropriate;
- provisions for effective involvement and participation by the learner, coupled with rapid and extensive feedback, where appropriate;
- wherever appropriate, a learning pace which is modified by the actions of the learner or which can be adjusted by the teacher based on diagnosed needs;
- a fair, reasonable, and clearly stated publisher's policy governing the replacement of defective or damaged program media such as tapes, diskettes, ROM cartridges, and the like;
- a publisher's preview policy which provides pre-purchase samples or copies for review and which encourages a well-informed software acquisition process by reading educators.

2. About hardware

Hardware should be durable, capable of producing highly legible text displays, and safe for use in a classroom situation. Hardware should be chosen that conforms to established classroom needs. Some characteristics to be aware of include, but are not limited to, the following:

- compatibility with classroom software appropriate to the curriculum;
- proven durability in classroom situations;
- clear, unambiguous instruction manuals appropriate for use by persons having a minimum of technical experience with computers;
- sufficient memory (RAM) capability to satisfy anticipated instructional software applications;
- availability of disk, tape, ROM cartridge, or other efficient and reliable data storage devices;
- screen displays which produce legible print, minimize glare, and which have the lowest possible screen radiation levels;
- a functional keyboard and the availability of other appropriate types of input devices;
- proven, accessible, and reasonably priced technical support from the manufacturer or distributor.

3. About staff development and training

Staff development programs should be available which encourage teachers to become intelligent users of technology in the reading classroom. Factors to consider include, but are not limited to, the following:
- study and practice with various applications of computer technology in the reading and language arts classroom;
- training which encourages thoughtful and informed evaluation, selection and integration of effective and appropriate teaching software into the reading and language arts classroom.

4. About equity

All persons, regardless of sex, ethnic group, socioeconomic status, or ability must have equality of access to the challenges and benefits of computer technology. Computer technology should be integrated into all classrooms and not be limited to scientific or mathematical applications.

5. About research

Research which assesses the impact of computer technology on all aspects of learning-to-read and reading to learn is essential.

6. About inappropriate use of technology

Computers should be used in meaningful and productive ways which relate clearly to instructional needs of students in the reading classroom. Educators must capitalize on the potential of this technology by insisting on its appropriate and meaningful use.

*Adapted from International Reading Association, Newark, Delaware.

Reading Break Survey – Teacher Survey

1. Give an estimate in percentage (multiples of 5) of overall participation by your class in the Reading Break:

   _____ %

2. Is the Reading Break beneficial to your students?

   Very Beneficial   Not at all Beneficial
       4   3   2   1

3. Do your students observe the Reading Break in your classroom?   ☐ Regularly
     ☐ Occasionally
     ☐ Seldom

4. Do you observe the Reading Break by modeling reading?   ☐ Regularly
     ☐ Occasionally
     ☐ Seldom

5. Would you like to see the Reading Break continued?   ☐ Yes   ☐ No

6. Do you see the supervision of students as part of your responsibility?   ☐ Yes   ☐ No

---

Directions to Teachers: The following survey is an informational tally of the uses of the Reading Break by the students. Please follow the instructions below to help us gather information about the Reading Break

During the Reading Break on (date), please take a few minutes in the middle of your reading, to unobtrusively glance around your room or supervision site and record on the following sheet what is happening during the Reading Break.

Please return the survey by _____.

Reading Break

Teacher: _____   **Date:** _____

No. of Students: _____   **Class:** _____

Total No. of Students Reading: _____

Total No. of Students not Reading: _____

Reading		Students Not Reading	
Reading Material	No. of Students	List Activity	No. of Students
Books	_____	_____	_____
Newspapers	_____	_____	_____
Magazines	_____	_____	_____
Other: (list)	_____	_____	_____
_____	_____		
_____	_____		

Reading Break Survey – Student Survey

		Grade:	9	10	11	12

1. Is reading useful or important to you?

☐ Very important
☐ Important
☐ Somewhat important
☐ Not very important
☐ Not at all important

2. Do you think daily reading practice can help you improve your reading?

☐ Yes
☐ No

3. What word describes your feeling toward reading?

☐ Enjoy
☐ Accept
☐ Tolerate
☐ Dislike
☐ Hate

4. What do you think of the Reading Break?

☐ Excellent idea
☐ O.K. idea
☐ Don't care
☐ Don't like it
☐ It's terrible

5. Do you come prepared to Reading Break?

☐ Always
☐ Usually
☐ Sometimes
☐ Never

6. Do you consistently use the time for silent reading?

☐ Every day
☐ 3-4 days per week
☐ 1-2 days per week
☐ Never

7. Are you reading a book now?

☐ Yes
☐ No

8. How often do you talk about something you've read?

☐ Often
☐ Occasionally
☐ Seldom
☐ Never

NAEP Reading Objectives, 1983-84

I. **Comprehends What is Read**

   A. Comprehends various types of written materials

   B. Comprehends materials read for a particular purpose

II. **Extends Comprehension**

   A. Analyzes what has been read

   B. Interprets what has been read

   C. Evaluates what has been read

III. **Manages the Reading Experience**

   A. Uses the structure and organization of text

   B. Uses Readers' Aids

   C. Shows flexibility in approach to reading

   D. Selects reading materials appropriate to the purpose

IV. **Values Reading**

   A. Values reading as a source of enjoyment

   B. Values reading to expand understanding and fulfill personal goals

   C. Values reading as a means of acquiring knowledge and learning new skills

   D. Values the cultural role of written language

Annotated Bibliography

The following list of publications was used to review the research and current practices for developing the model and framework described in the *Guide to Curriculum Planning in Reading*. Readers can refer to these publications for complete descriptions of the research entries cited in sections 1 and 2 and throughout the guide.

Becoming A Nation of Readers: The Report of the Commission on Reading, ed. by R. C. Anderson, E. H. Hubert, J. A. Scott, I. Wilkinson, Champaign, Illinois 61820-81774, 1985.
Summarizes the current knowledge about reading and offers practical solutions to improve reading instruction.

Becoming a Strategic Reader, by Scott G. Paris, Marjorie Lipson, and Karen Wixson, 3210 School of Education, University of Michigan, Ann Arbor, MI 48109.
An important aspect of learning to read is understanding how to use strategies to aid comprehension. Strategies are self-directed plans for learning that include knowledge about reading as a thinking activity, as well as control over one's actual reading performance. This paper examines aspects of knowledge and motivation that are critical to becoming a strategic reader.

Becoming Readers in a Complex Society. ed. by A. Purves and Olive Niles, 83rd Yearbook of the National Society for the Study of Education, University of Chicago Press, Chicago, Illinois, 1984.
This report of the National Society gives particular attention to instruction in reading in middle grades and beyond.

Comprehension and Teaching: Research Reviews, ed. by J. Guthrie, IRA, Newark, Delaware, 1982.
This volume includes readings from a broad perspective for bridging the gap between understanding the reading process and instructional practice.

Comprehension Instruction: Perspectives and Suggestions, by Gerald G. Duffy, Laura Roehler, and Jana Mason, Longman Inc., 1560 Broadway, New York, NY 10036, 1984.
This book represents a cooperative effort between the Center for the Study of Reading and the Institute for Research on Teaching to discover the best methods for teaching students to comprehend. The book emphasizes the importance of the teacher as the decision maker in the classroom rather than the basal reader manual, and it shows teachers how to teach students to become strategic readers.

Handbook of Reading Research, ed. by D. Pearson, New York, Longman, 1984.
This recent edition provides a comprehensive analysis and interpretation of the current research in reading.

Learning to Read in American Schools: Basal Readers and Content Texts, ed. by Richard C. Anderson, Jean Osborn, and Robert J. Tierney, Lawrence Erlbaum Associates, 365 Broadway, Hillsdale, New Jersey 07642, 1984.

This book is essential for any reading library. It is written by researchers connected with the Center for the Study of Reading, and it outlines many of the important areas of concern: direct instruction, basal readers, the use of workbooks, story structure, content-area textbooks, background knowledge, and metacognition.

Reader Meets Author Bridging the Gap: A Psycholinguistic and Socialinguistic, by Judy Langer and M. T. Smith-Burke, Newark, Delaware, IRA, 1982.
Translates the present view of reading into many worthwhile practices.

Reading Comprehension Assessment: A Cognitive Basis, by Peter H. Johnston, International Reading Association, 800 Barksdale Road, Newark, Delaware, 1983.
Peter Johnston has asked some revolutionary questions about reading assessment: What should we assess? What can we assess? How should we assess? All of these assume that current means of assessment are inadequate because they are based on faulty premises.

Reading Comprehension: From Research to Practice, ed. by Judith Orasanu, Lawrence Erlbaum Associates, 365 Broadway, Hillsdale, NJ 07642, 1985.
This book captures the significance of the National Institute of Education's efforts to investigate the nature of reading comprehension and to make suggestions for improving reading comprehension.

Reading: The Patterning of Complex Behavior, by Marie Clay. Heinemann Educational Books, Aucklund, N. Zealand, 1978.
This book focuses on the developmental patterns of reading behavior with emphasis on the emergent reader and early stages.

Secondary School Reading: What Research Reveals for Classroom Practice, ed. by Allen Berger and H. Alan Robinson, ERIC Clearinghouse on Reading and Communication Skills, 1111 Kenyon Road, Urbana, IL 61801, 1982.
This is currently the best book on content-area reading programs. It contains excellent articles on all aspects of high school reading, and provides guidance in developing a comprehensive high school reading program.

Stages of Reading Development, by Jeanne S. Chall, McGraw-Hill Book Company, 1221 Avenue of the Americas, New York, NY 10020, 1983.
One of the more controversial books to appear recently, Chall's book argues that reading is a developmental process that can be characterized by six stages: Pre-reading; initial reading or decoding; confirmation, fluency, ungluing from print; reading for learning the new; multiple viewpoints; construction and reconstruction—a world view.

Understanding Reading Comprehension, ed. by James Flood, International Reading Association, 800 Barksdale Road, Newark, Delaware, 1984.
This book highlights the recent research on reading as a process.

The Reading Report Card–(NAEP, 1985), Educational Testing Service, Princeton, New Jersey.
The National Assessment of Education Progress reports trends in reading from 1970-1984.

Bibliography/Scope and Sequence

Word Meaning and Analysis

Chomsky, Carol. "After Decoding: What?" *Language Arts* (March 1976).

Cross, Mary M. *What You Always Wanted to Know About Research Findings: Reading Comprehension.* Washington, D.C.: National Institute of Education, 1984.

Durkin, Dolores. *Strategies for Identifying Words.* Boston: Allyn and Bacon, 1976.

Durr, William K. "Developing Word Recognition Skills—An Interview." *Wisconsin State Reading Association Journal* 27 (Fall 1982).

Graves, M. F. "Selecting Vocabulary to Teach in the Intermediate and Secondary Grades." In *Promoting Reading Comprehension,* edited by J. Flood. Newark, DE: International Reading Association, 1984.

Johnson, Dale and P. David Pearson. *Teaching Reading Vocabulary.* New York: Holt, Rinehart and Winston, 1984.

McConaughy, Stephanie H. "Word Recognition and Word Meaning in the Total Reading Process." *Language Arts* 55 (November/December 1978).

Samuels, S. Jay. "Modes of Word Recognition." In *Theoretical Models and Processes of Reading,* edited by Harvey Singer and Robert B. Ruddell. Newark, DE.: International Reading Association, 1976.

Narrative and Expository

Narrative

Golden, J. "Children's Concept of Story in Reading and Writing." *The Reading Teacher* 37 (March 1984).

Gordon, C. and C. Baum. "Using Story Schema as an Aid to Reading and Writing." *The Reading Teacher* 37 (November 1983).

Jett-Simpson, M. "The Classroom Teacher as an Action Researcher: Story Mapping." *Wisconsin State Reading Association Journal* 27 (1983).

_____. "Writing Stories Using Models Structures: The Circle Story." *Language Arts* 58 (1981).

McConaughy, S. "Developmental Changes in Story Comprehension and Levels of Questioning." *Language Arts* 59 (1982).

Expository

Anderson, T. H. and B. B. Armbruster. *Readable Textbooks or Selecting a Textbook Is Not Like Buying a Pair of Shoes*. Champaign, IL: Center for the Study of Reading, 1984.

_____. *Content Area Textbooks*. (Reading Education Report No. 23). Champaign, IL: Center for the Study of Reading, 1981.

Early, M. and D. Sawyer. *Reading to Learn in Grades 5-12*. New York: Harcourt Brace Jovanovich, 1984.

Flood, J., ed. *Understanding Reading Comprehension*. Newark, DE: International Reading Association, 1984.

Meyer, B. J. "Organizational Patterns in Prose and Their Use in Reading." *Reading Research: Studies and Applications*, edited by M. L. Kamil and A. J. Moe. Twenty-eighth Yearbook of the National Reading Conference, 1979.

Otto, W. and S. White. *Reading Expository Material*. New York: Harcourt Brace Jovanovich, 1982.

Critical Reading/Thinking

Adler, M. M. and C. Van Doren. *How to Read a Book*. New York: Simon and Schuster, 1972.

Altick, R. D. *Preface to Critical Thinking*. New York: Holt, Rinehart and Winston, 1960.

Hudgins, B. *Learning and Thinking: A Primer for Teachers*. Itasca, IL: F. E. Peacock, 1977.

King, M., B. D. Ellinger, and W. Wolf, eds. *Critical Reading*. Philadelphia: J. B. Lippincott, 1967.

Pearson, P. D. and D. D. Johnson. *Teaching Reading Comprehension*. New York: Holt, Rinehart and Winston, 1984.

Smith, R. J. and T. C. Barrett. *Teaching Reading in the Middle Grades*. Reading, MA: Addison-Wesley, 1976.

Responding in Writing

Applebee, Arthur N. and Judith A. Langer. "Instructional Scaffolding: Reading and Writing as Natural Language Activities." *Language Arts* 60 (February 1983).

Applebee, Arthur N., Fran Lehr, and Anne Auten. "Learning to Write in the Secondary School: How and Where." *English Journal* (September 1981).

Bibliography for Scope and Sequence

Chall, Jeanne S. and Vicki A. Jacobs. "Writing and Reading in the Elementary Grades: Developmental Trends Among Low SES Children." *Language Arts* 60 (May 1983).

Eckhoff, Barbara. "How Reading Affects Children's Writing." *Language Arts* 60 (May 1983).

Goodman, Kenneth and Yetta Goodman. "Reading and Writing Relationships: Pragmatic Functions." *Language Arts* 60 (May 1983).

Graves, Donald. *Writing: Teachers and Children at Work.* Exeter, NH: Heineman Educational Books, 1983.

Hailey, Jack. *Teaching Writing K-8.* Berkeley, CA: Instructional Laboratory, University of California, 1978.

Hennings, Dorothy Grant. "A Writing Approach to Reading Comprehension - Schema Theory in Action." *Language Arts* 59 (January 1982).

Holt, Suzanne L. and JoAnne L. Vacca. "Reading With a Sense of Writer: Writing With a Sense of Reader." *Language Arts* 58 (November/December 1981).

Newkirk, Thomas. "Young Writers as Critical Readers." *Language Arts* 59 (May 1982).

Sealey, Leonard, Nancy Sealey, and Marcia Millmore. *Children's Writing: An Approach for the Primary Grades.* Newark, DE: International Reading Association, 1979.

Smith, Frank. "Reading Like a Writer." *Language Arts* 60 (May 1983).

Squire, James R. "Composing and Comprehending: Two Sides of the Same Basic Process." *Language Arts* 60 (May 1983).

Tierney, Robert J. and P. David Pearson. "Toward a Composing Model of Reading." *Language Arts* 60 (May 1983).

Attitudes and Interests

Alexander, J. Estill and Ronald Claude Filler. *Attitudes and Reading.* Newark, DE: International Reading Association, 1978.

Allington, R. I. "Poor Readers Don't Get to Read Much." *Language Arts* 57 (1980).

Bamberger, R. *Promoting the Reading Habit.* Paris: Unesco Press, 1975.

Burrows, Alvina Treut. "Building Lifetime Reading Habits in an Individualized Reading Program." In *Elementary Reading Instruction: Selected Materials*, 2d ed., edited by Althea Beery, et. al. Boston: Allyn and Bacon, 1974.

Diani, Alfred J., ed. *Motivating Reluctant Readers*. Newark, DE: International Reading Association, 1981.

Dietrich, D. M. and V. H. Mathews, eds. *Development of Lifetime Reading Habits*. Newark, DE: International Reading Association, 1968.

Fredericks, Anthony D. "Developing Positive Reading Attitudes." *The Reading Teacher* 36 (October 1982).

Quandt, Ivan J. *Teaching Reading: A Human Process*. Chicago: Rand McNally College Publishing Co., 1977.

Strickler, Darryl J., ed. *The Affective Dimension of Reading*. Bloomington, IN: Indiana University Publications, 1977.

Veatch, Jeannette. *For the Love of Teaching*. Encino, CA: International Center for Educational Development, 1973.

Veatch, Jeannette. *Key Words to Reading: The Language Experience Approach Begins*. Columbus, OH: Charles E. Merrill Publishing Company, 1979.

Bibliography/Strategic Behavior

Babbs, P. and A. Moe. "Metacognition: A Key for Independent Learning From Text." *The Reading Teacher* 36 (1983).

Beck, I. L. and M. McKeown. "Learning Words Well—A Program to Enhance Vocabulary and Comprehsion." *The Reading Teacher* 36 (1983).

Bridge, C. A., P. N. Winograd, and D. Haley. "Using Predictable Materials vs. Preprimer to Teach Beginning Sight Words." *The Reading Teacher* 36 (1983).

Davidson, J. L. "The Group Mapping Activity for Instruction in Reading and Writing." *The Reading Teacher* 26 (1982).

Davey, B. "Think Aloud—Modeling the Cognitive Processes of Reading Comprehension." *Journal of Reading* 27 (1983).

Fitzgerald, J. "Helping Readers Gain Self-Control Over Reading Comprehension." *The Reading Teacher* 37 (1983).

Fowler, G. L. "Developing Comprehension Skills in Primary Students Through the Use of Story Frames." *The Reading Teacher* 36 (1982).

Gipe, J. "Use of a Relevant Context Helps Kids Learn New Word Meanings." *The Reading Teacher* 33 (1980).

Hanson, J. "An Inferential Comprehension Strategy for Use with Primary Grade Children." *The Reading Teacher* 34 (1981).

Langer, J. and M. T. Smith-Burke. *Reader Meets Author/Bridging the Gap.* Newark, DE: International Reading Association, 1982.

Merlin, S.B. and F. Rogers. "Direct Teaching Strategies." *The Reading Teacher* 35 (1981).

Myers, M. and S. G. Paris. "Children's Metacognitive Knowledge About Reading." *Journal of Educational Psychology* 70 (1978).

Paris, S. G. and M. Myers. "Comprehension Monitoring in Good and Poor Readers." *Journal of Reading Behavior* 13 (1981).

Paris, S. G., Evelyn R. Oka, and Ann Marie DeBritto. "Beyond Decoding: Synthesis of Research on Reading Comprehension." *Educational Leadership* 8 (October 1983).

Paris, S. G., Marjorie Y. Lipson, and Karen K. Wixson. "Becoming a Strategic Reader." *Contemporary Educational Psychology* 8 (1983).

Pitts, M. "Comprehension Monitoring, Definition and Practice." *Journal of Reading* 26 (1983).

Bibliography/Comprehension Instruction

Allington, Richard. "The Reading Instruction Provided Readers of Differing Reading Abilities." *Elementary School Journal* 6 (May 1983).

Beck, I., R. Omanson, and M. McKeown. "An Instructional Redesign of Reading Lessons: Effects on Comprehension." *Reading Research Quarterly* 17 (1982).

Brown, A. "Learning How to Learn from Reading. *Reader Meets Author/Bridging the Gap,* edited By J. Langer and M. T. Smith-Burke. Newark, DE: International Reading Association, (1982).

Durkin, D. "Is There a Match Between What Elementary Teachers Do and What Basal Reader Manuals Recommend?" *The Reading Teacher* 37 (1984).

_____. "Reading Comprehension Instruction in Five Basal Reader Series." *Reading Research Quarterly* 16 (1981).

_____. "What Classroom Observations Reveal about Reading Comprehension Instruction." *Reading Research Quarterly* 14 (1979).

Fitzgerald, J. and D. Spiegel. "Enhancing Children's Reading Comprehension through Instruction in Narrative Structure." *Journal of Reading Behavior* 15 (1983).

Hansen, J. "An Inferential Comprehension Strategy for Use with Primary Grade Children." *The Reading Teacher* 34 (1981).

Jett-Simpson, Mary. "The Classroom Teacher as an Action Researcher: Generalizations for Guiding Comprehension." *Wisconsin State Reading Journal* 27 (1983).

Marr, M. and K. Gormley. "Children's Recall of Familiar and Unfamiliar Text." *Reading Research Quarterly* 18 (1982).

McConaughy, S. "Developmental Changes in Story Comprehension Levels of Questioning." *Language Arts* 59 (1982).

Moore, D. W., J. E. Readence, and R. J. Rickelman. *Prereading Activities for Content Area Reading and Learning.* Newark, DE: International Reading Association, 1982.

Nichols, J. N. "Using Prediction to Increase Content Area Interest and Understanding." *Journal of Reading* 27 (1983).

Olsen, M. W. "A Dash of Story Grammar and . . . Presto! A Book Report." *The Reading Teacher* 37 (1983).

Pearson, D. "Changing the Face of Reading Comprehension Instruction." *The Reading Teacher* 38 (April 1985).

Raphael, T. E. *QARS Revisited.* Newark, DE: International Reading Association, 1985.

_____. "Question-answering Strategies for Children." *The Reading Teacher* 36 (1982).

Rosenshine, B. "Content Time and Direct Instruction. *Research on Teaching: Concepts, Findings and Implications*, edited by H. Walberg and P. Peterson. Berkeley, CA: McCutchan Publishing Co., 1979.

Rumelhart, D. E. *Toward an Interactive Model for Reading* (Technical Report No. 56) San Diego: University of California, Center for Human Information Processing, 1977.

Santa, C., and B. Hayes. *Children's Prose Comprehension.* Newark, DE: International Reading Association, 1981.

Spiegel, D. L. "Six Alternatives to the Directed Reading Activity. *The Reading Teacher* 34 (1981).

Stevens, K. "Can We Improve Reading by Teaching Background Information?" *Journal of Reading* 25 (1982).

Steward, O. and E. Tei. "Some Implications of Metacognition for Reading Instruction. *Journal of Reading* 27 (1983).

Swaby, B. "Varying the Ways You Teach Reading with Basal Stories." *The Reading Teacher* 35 (1982).

Taylor, B. M. and L. Nosbush. "Oral Reading for Meaning: A Technique for Improving Word Identification Skills." *The Reading Teacher* 37 (1983).

Vaughan, J. G. Castle, K. Gilbert, and M. Love. "Varied Approaches to Preteaching Vocabulary." *New Inquiries in Reading Research and Instruction*, edited by J. Niles and L. Harris. Rochester, NY: National Reading Conference, 1982.

Whaley, J. F. "Story Grammars and Reading Instruction." *The Reading Teacher* 34 (1981).

Wilson, C. R. Teaching Reading Comprehension by Connecting the Known to the New. *The Reading Teacher* 36 (1983).

Wittrock, M. "Writing and Teaching of Reading." *Language Arts* 60 (1982).

Wixson, K. K. "Questions about a Text: What You Ask about is What Children Learn." *The Reading Teacher* 37 (1983).

Wood, K. D. and N. Robinson. "Vocabulary, Language, and Prediction: A Prereading Strategy." *The Reading Teacher* 36 (1983).

Bibliography/Staff Development

Bishop, Leslee J. *Staff Development and Instructional Improvement: Plans and Procedures.* Boston: Allyn and Bacon, 1976.

Shanker, James L. *Guidelines for Successful Reading Staff Development.* Newark, DE: International Reading Association, 1982.

Smith, Richard J., Wayne Otto, and Lee Hansen. *The School Reading Program.* Boston: Houghton, Mifflin Co., 1978.

Sparks, George Mohlman. "Synthesis of Research of Staff Development for Effective Teaching." *Educational Leadership* (November 1983).

Taylor, Bob L., and Robert C. McKean. "News Notes: Checkpoints for Improved Inservice." *Educational Leadership* (February 1982).

Bibliography/Helpful Guides for Teaching Reading

Allen, R., K. Brown, and J. Yatvin. *Learning Language Through Communication: A Functional Perspective.* Belmont, CA: Wadsworth Publishing, 1985.

Bragstad, Bernice and Sharyn Stumpf. *Study Skills and Motivation: A Guidebook for Teachers.* Boston: Allyn and Bacon, 1982.

Clay, Marie. *Early Detection of Reading Difficulties.* Edison, NJ: Heineman Educational Books, 1983.

Durkin, Dolores. *Teaching Young Children to Read.* 3rd ed. Boston: Allyn and Bacon, 1978.

Early, Margaret and O. J. Sawyer. *Reading to Learn in Grades 5-12.* Chicago: Harcourt Brace Jovanovich, 1984.

Graham, G. K. and H. A. Robinson. *Study Skills Handbook.* Newark, DE: International Reading Association, 1984.

Hall, Mary Anne. *Teaching Reading as a Language Experience.* 3rd ed. Columbus, OH: Charles E. Merrill Publishing Co., 1981.

Hardt, U. H. *Teaching Reading With the Other Language Arts.* Newark, DE: International Reading Association, 1983.

Harker, John, ed. *Classroom Strategies for Secondary Reading.* 2nd ed. Newark, DE: International Reading Association, 1985.

Hennings, D. G. *Teaching Communication and Reading Skills in the Content Areas.* Bloomington, IN: Phi Delta Kappa, 1982.

Herber, Harold. *Teaching Reading in the Content Areas.* 2nd ed. Englewood Cliffs, NJ: Prentice-Hall, Inc., 1978.

Holdaway, Don. *Independence in Reading.* Sydney, Australia. Ashton Scholastic Co.

Jaggar, A. and M. Trika Burke-Smith, eds. *Observing the Language Learner.* Newark, DE: International Reading Association, 1985.

Johnson, Dale D. and P. David Pearson. *Teaching Reading Vocabulary.* New York: Holt, Rinehart and Winston, 1984.

Lapp, D. *Making Reading Possible Through Effective Classroom Management.* Newark, DE: International Reading Association, 1980.

Lapp, D. and J. Hood. *Teaching Reading to Every Child.* New York: MacMillan Publication Co., 1983.

McNeil, John D. *Reading Comprehension: New Directions for Classroom Practice.* Glenview, IL: Scott Foresman & Co., 1984.

Moffett, J. and B. J. Wagner. *Student Centered—Language Arts and Reading—K-13.* 3rd ed. Geneva, IL: Houghton Mifflin Co., 1983.

Moore, David W., John E. Readence, and Robert J. Richelman. *Prereading Activities for Content Area Reading and Learning.* Newark, DE: International Reading Association, 1982.

Orasanu, Judith, ed. *Reading Comprehension: From Research to Practice.* Hillsdale, NJ: Lawrence Erlbaum Associates, Inc., 1985.

Pearson, P. D. and D. D. Johnson. *Teaching Reading Comprehension.* New York: Holt, Rinehart and Winston, 1978.

Roe, B . D., B. D. Stoodt, and P. C. Burns. *Secondary School Reading Instruction. The Content Areas.* 2nd ed. Geneva, IL: Houghton Mifflin Co., 1985.

Samuels, S. Jay, ed. *What Research Has to Say about Reading Instruction.* Newark, DE: International Reading Association, 1978.

Schell, L. S., ed. *Diagnostic and Criterion Referenced Reading Tests: Review and Evaluation.* Newark, DE: International Reading Association, 1980.

Stauffer, Russell A. *The Language Experience Approach to the Teaching of Reading.* 2nd ed. New York: Harper and Row, 1980.

Swaby, Barbara E. R. *Teaching and Learning Reading: A Pragmatic Approach.* Boston: Little, Brown & Co., 1984.

Tierney, R. J., J. E. Readence, and E. K. Desher. *Reading Strategies and Practices: Guide for Improving Instruction.* Boston: Allyn and Bacon, 1985.

Veatch, Jeanette. *Reading in the Elementary School.* 2nd ed. New York: John Wiley and Sons, 1978.

Book Lists and Resources

Cooperative Children's Book Center
4290 Helen C. White Hall
600 North Park Street
Madison, WI 53706

The Horn Book
Park Square Building
31 St. James Square
Boston, MA 02116

The Great Books Foundation
35 E. Wacker Drive, Suite 2300
Chicago, IL 60601

Children's Books
(an annual bibliography)
Library of Congress
Washington, DC 20005

Adventuring with Books
National Council of Teachers of English
111 Kenyon Road
Urbana, IL 61801

Annual Book Lists
International Reading Association
800 Barksdale Road
P.O. Box 8139
Newark, DE 19711

American Library Association
50 East Huron Street
Chicago, IL 60611

Children's Book Council
67 Irving Place
New York, NY 10003

**Wisconsin State Reading
Association Journal**
4809 Sternberg Avenue
Schofield, WI 54475-2835

**Council on Interracial
Books for Children**
1841 Broadway
New York, NY 10023-7648

**Center for the Study of
Children's Literature**
Simmons College
300 The Fenway
Boston, MA. 02115

Organizations

Wisconsin State Reading Association
4461 Quarry Circle
Wisconsin Rapids, WI 54496-8817

International Reading Association
(IRA) Publications
800 Barksdale Road
P.O. Box 8139
Newark, DE 19711

North Central Regional
Educational Laboratory
1900 Spring Road, Suite 300
Oakbrook, IL 60521-1480

National Council of Teachers of
English (NCTE)
111 Kenyon Road
Urbana, IL 61801

National Assessment of
Educational Progress
Box 2923
Princeton, NJ 08541

Association for Supervision and
Curriculum Development (ASCD)
225 North Washington Street
Alexandria, VA 22314

Center for the Study of Reading
University of Illinois at Urbana-
Champaign
51 Gerty Drive
Champaign, IL 61820

Institute for Research on Teaching
Michigan State University
East Lansing, MI 48824

Wisconsin Council of Teachers
of English
Appleton Area School District
P.O. Box 2019
Appleton, WI 54913

Center for Education Research
University of Wisconsin
1025 West Johnson Street
Madison, WI 53706

Research and Development Center
University of Pittsburgh
Pittsburgh, PA 15261

*America will become a
nation of readers when
verified practices of the
best teachers in the best
schools can be
introduced throughout
the country.
–Becoming a Nation
of Readers*